WOUNDED DOVE

A TRUE STORY OF COURAGE, FAITH, AND LOVE

VIRGINIA HESLINGA

3clocks
publications

publications

Published by 3 Clocks Publications

Wounded Dove: A True Story of Courage, Faith, and Love
Second Edition

eBook ISBN: 979-8-9883543-4-5

Paperback ISBN: 979-8-9883543-3-8

Hardback ISBN: 979-8-9883543-5-2

Audiobook ISBN: 979-8-9883543-6-9

Edited by Carolyn Allard

Cover and Interior Design by Gordon Saunders

Publisher's Note:

This is a work of creative fiction based on real people and places in Worcester and Holden, Massachusetts. The author has presented the events to the best of her abilities. While all the incidents in the book are true, names of people have been changed to protect privacy. For this reason, the book falls into the historical fiction category.

PRAISE FOR WOUNDED DOVE

"*Wounded Dove* will make people reflect on their unpleasant personal and family predicaments and then look up to God and thank Him for taking them through those situations and forgiving them when asked, releasing their guilt and anguish."
   –Lieutenant Fred Lussier, Massachusetts State Police (ret.)

"*Wounded Dove* takes readers on an emotional life journey of triumphs, heartaches, and the enduring legacy of family. Based on true events, the novel beautifully paints a picture of what life was like in the early 1900s in Worcester County. Readers will appreciate the local landmarks and history skillfully tied in with Annelise's story of survival. Being rooted in reality and research, makes Annelise's perspective all the more compelling for modern audiences who will root for her, cry for her, and pay respect to a complicated life well lived."
   –Sloane M. Perron, freelance writer

"I sit here with tears on my cheeks. I just read *Wounded Dove* in one day, and it is magnificent."

–A. W. Ciriacy, Jr., MA, Compliance Officer, Minnesota Department of Education (ret)

Wounded Dove written by Virginia Heslinga chronicles the complex integration of a Danish immigrant farming family into a small town in central Massachusetts in the early twentieth century. Uniquely, much of the story is framed by the life experience of one of the daughters, who was disabled as a young girl by polio. Based on information provided by the family, *Wounded Dove* is compelling and engaging, and occupies a distinctive place in the tradition of U.S. immigration literature.

–Dr. Barbara Driscoll de Alvarado, Associate Professor of Humanities, Anna Maria College, Paxton, MA

This book is dedicated to some of the generous women in my life who loved God and helped every wounded person they met.

Idalene Steele Bishop
1897-1981

Esther Martin Wood
1909-2007

Virginia Riposta Pietoso
1920-2008

Katherine Aegesen Bishop Riposta
1932-2020

Joanne Lee D'Aria
1950-2020

WOUNDED DOVE

AMERICAN DOMESTICATION

"All available evidence shows that from the time primitive man first domesticated animals, the pigeon (dove) was regarded as the highest of all speechless creatures and was an integral part of the life of man. This evidence begins about 5000 years ago with carvings on stone and statues in buried cities and subsequently in writings on parchment." **W.M. Levi, *Encyclopedia of Pigeons***

Adia Joren's second Christmas in America found her trying to make sure her three little children were warm through weeks of snow and bitter cold. Any time they had to step outside, the wind and freezing temperatures ripped into their flesh like a dry ice knife. She listened to the soulless wind as she kneaded bread dough and watched the children.

No longer toddlers, her daughters, Ingelise and Hanne played well together. Ingelise had been born in November 1899, and Hanne in April 1901. They were so close they acted like twins. They tolerated their baby sister, Annelise, but often ignored her. Annelise had entered the world in August 1905, a financially tough year for the family.

God had seen the family through their greatest scarcity. Without his help, Adia doubted her endurance could have persevered as an immigrant wife and mother of three small children. There were too many daily challenges for body, soul, and spirit. Adia's mind and heart filled with thankfulness. God had given her spirit rest while her body worked and she felt strong.

Her husband, Asa, worked harder, and she prayed daily for him as he left before dawn for a full day of hard labor. They had not yet had ten years of marriage together, but Adia could not imagine life without him. He helped her to have hope in the future and trust in God.

A child's cry broke Adia's reverie. Ingelise and Hanne shared a chair and a book and would not let Annelise climb into their laps. Adia wondered if Hanne would be more generous to Annelise when Ingelise was at school in the fall. Ingelise seemed resentful of the new sister, yet she accepted Hanne. Adia sighed with a shiver as she prayed Hanne would be interested and friendly to Annelise. Hanne's eyes displayed her adoration of her big sister, Ingelise.

Annelise crawled and walked from chair to chair. Adia knew what it felt like to want to hold onto something. In a new country, learning a new language, perceived as a foreigner—all the challenges made her feel insecure. The Lord and Asa encouraged her each day.

Their youngest child, Annelise possessed a strong desire to belong. She tried to stay near her sisters. She mimicked them. When she couldn't crawl after them, her eyes followed them in everything they did.

All they needed today was to stay warm in the kitchen.

Adia could tell that Ingelise understood the kitchen was the best place for play. She led Hanne in setting up imaginary places and journeys around the kitchen with some tin toys Asa bought in Worcester.

Asa was concerned about no insulation in their small rented farmhouse. The owner would not give them an option to buy the farm, so Asa was reluctant to spend money on repairs. He stacked plenty of firewood within her reach. Both bedrooms were upstairs over the kitchen, and Asa had vented them to allow the kitchen heat to float above. That helped, but when the wind blew and the temperature fell far below freezing, the vents weren't enough to keep their rented house warm.

Adia saw through a window—almost entirely frosted— more snow falling like feathers shaken out of a huge pillow. Asa tended their cow, horse, goats, and chickens in the barn. The night would be severely cold, colder than a December night should be. This month seemed the coldest since she had arrived in America, even colder than winters in Denmark.

Adia formed the kneaded dough into loaves by rote. She had made bread in Denmark since a young girl. In 1896, Asa had arrived in America and sent for her in 1897. They'd lived almost ten years in America. Asa's goal remained to own land in America before he was thirty. He was close. She had admired and respected him before she loved him.

They saved for their farm. Asa was convinced owning good land—high and dry but near water—was the smartest earthly investment. He continued to look at available land to know the opportunities. He worked three jobs constantly to pay bills and save for the farm.

Their rented small farm in Grafton was too far from Asa's work in Worcester. He said Grafton was a strong community to live in, but trekking to his Worcester jobs sapped his energy. Grafton afforded them a chance to have a small house and barnlike shed. They had moved into the house just weeks before Annelise was born.

Asa worked seventeen to twenty hours a day, except Sundays. On Sundays he brushed the horse and cared for their cow, goats, and chickens. He drove the family to and from church. He looked so serious, weighted by the responsibilities of his family and dreams. Aida longed to see more joy in Asa.

Adia slid the bread pans into the oven beside the fireplace. A warm kitchen and the smell of fresh bread would please Asa when he came inside.

While brushing the flour from her hands, Adia heard the first signs of sleepy tiredness in the girls' voices. Hanne whined. If she read to them, they would cuddle and settle. Adia sat in the armchair and picked up the book, *The Friendly Beasts*, a sweet look at the Christmas story through the animals' eyes.

The girls squealed with delight and hurried to climb onto her lap. Adia edged to one side for Ingelise to sit and hold the book while she scooped Annelise and Hanne onto her lap.

"Mama," Ingelise begged, "Read it, read it."

"Please, please," Hanne agreed.

Their enthusiasm energized Adia. The book contained beautiful pictures with leather binding, a treasure like her parents' beloved books in Denmark. The book, beyond anything they could afford, had been a gift from one of Asa's wealthy customers. Asa had built a playhouse for the rich man's children.

The playhouse was as snug and secure as real houses. Asa did quality work, but on this project, he applied his craft for safety and strength. Asa loved children as the precious gift of

God. He said children were a sign God had hope for mankind.

Adia looked toward the door again. The howling wind chilled her soul. She wished Asa would come inside for hot food and drink while she read to the girls. They saw their papa less than his customers did.

A thump on the porch made Adia's heart beat faster at she thought Asa might appear, but he did not.

Adia settled the girls in her lap so they could see the book.

"All right, girls," she said. "Ready?" Adia kept her arms around them all because Ingelise proudly held the picture book and turned the pages. They knew the words from listening to them over and over. Asa said the poem was actually a carol from England's Middle Ages. If the book disappeared, she could still provide them with the sweet story.

The Friendly Beasts

Jesus, our brother, kind and good,
was humbly born in a stable rude,
And the friendly beasts around Him stood;
Jesus, our brother kind and good.
"I," said the donkey, shaggy and brown.
"I carried His mother up hill and down;
I carried her safely to Bethlehem town;
"I," said the cow, all white and red,
I gave Him my manger for His bed;
I gave Him my hay to pillow His head;
I", said the cow, all white and red.
"I,"said the sheep with curly horn,
"I gave Him my wool for His blanket warm.
He wore my coat on Christmas morn.

I", said the sheep with curly horn.
"I," said the dove from the rafters high,
"Cooed Him to sleep, that He should not cry.
We cooed Him to sleep, my mate and I.
I", said the dove from the rafters high.
And every beast by some good spell,
In the stable dark was glad to tell
Of the gift they gave Immanuel.

They girls felt completely relaxed as Adia finished reading to them. The bodies, bundled in warm clothes, were still, warm, scented of childhood, redolent with sleepiness. The beautiful pictures and gentle repetitious rhymes entranced them as much as her voice did. She took the book slowly from Ingelise's little hands.

The clock from Denmark ticked, and the wood crackled and hissed in the stove. All else was quiet. Their custom after reading was to sit still until Adia kissed them each on the head. Gently she placed her lips on each silky crown. With her kiss, they all giggled and moved.

The final preparations for bed were familiar. Ingelise slowly slipped off her mother's lap to the wide pumpkin-pine floorboards. Hanne followed quickly and took Ingelise's hand. Both girls went to pick up their hot flannel-covered bricks and carried them in their skirts up the stairs to their bedroom. Their bed with a cedar chest at its foot and Annelise's crib on one side, filled the entire room.

Adia carried Annelise as she walked behind Ingelise and Hanne. The girls put the hot, wrapped bricks under the covers. The sheets would be warm by the time they changed into their night clothes. They hurriedly dressed, leaving on their warm socks Adia helped Annelise undress and into the warmth of the bunting she wore to bed.

The three girls hurried into bed after the chill of using the chamber pot and then washing their hands in the porcelain bowl. Most winter mornings, a light crust of ice covered the water. Ingelise and Hanne lay beneath the down-filled quilt over the double, flannel blanket and flannel sheets. The bricks did warm the bed. Then some good-natured pushing and giggling accompanied Ingelise and Hanne settling into bed

Adia put a blanket over Annelise and tucked the soft down-filled blanket around her. Leaning down, she kissed the toddler's brow, then turned to fling herself upon her other daughters. She squashed them with a hug and gave each a kiss.

Then Adia sat on the edge of the bed and sang to her daughters. She always sang a Danish lullaby and a hymn before they slept. She wanted them to hear their ancestors' language even if they would never know it enough to converse in it. These children she and Asa had produced were Americans, but she wanted them to value their parents' homeland.

Visselulle, min lire, Visselulle, min lire, (Sleep my little one)
Havde jeg suadanne fire (Had I now such four)
Fire-og-tyve i hver en Vraa (Four and twenty in a row)
Saa skulde alle vore Vugger gaa, (Then should all the cradles go.)
Visselulle, min lire! Visselulle, min lire! (Lullaby my baby.)

Adia sang in Danish and then in English, and finished in Danish. She hoped her girls would hear the words often so they could sing them. As the Danish words floated away, Adia sang the last song of the evening.

Since her girls had all been born in America, the last song

was in English. Most importantly the hymn reminded them they were loved by the One who loved best, the One who created them and would always be there with them and for them.

Jesus loves me! This I know,
for the Bible tells me so. Little ones to him belong;
they are weak, but He is strong.
Yes, Jesus loves me! Yes, Jesus loves you!
Yes, Jesus loves us! The Bible tells us so.

They were asleep before she finished the song. The snow swirled outside their window, but their beds were soft and warm. Adia ran her fingers lightly through their thick hair, like Asa's. She kissed them once more, then carried the chamber pot downstairs, along with the pewter-based oil lamp.

The wind moaned. Dear Asa was still working in the barn. *Please, God, bring him inside soon.* He worked too hard—but so often there seemed to be no other choice.

Adia felt sleepy but the scent of bread invaded her thoughts. The bread—a mixture of oatmeal and wheat flour—was done to a golden brown. She turned the loaves out on wire cooling racks and put the kettle on the iron stove. She had honey for the bread.

The mantle clock of dark cherry wood carved with leaves —a wedding present brought from Denmark—chimed half past eight. Asa always worked late to fix or build.

Adia lifted her woolen shawl from the back of a wooden chair. Just as she wrapped it around her shoulders, she heard Asa stomp the snow from his boots on the back porch. Letting her shawl fall, she hurried to greet him, grateful for him and their sweet girls.

Only a week later, when the wind-chill temperatures had moderated, the girls showed symptoms of sickness. Asa said all over Worcester a sickness seemed to turning up that could affect any age. Adia watched the girls carefully and felt fear when she saw how quickly the girls had succumbed to listlessness. They had no desire for food or stories. She could hardly get them to drink water.

Asa asked, "How are you feeling? Do you have a fever?"

Adia pressed the back of her long-fingered hand against her forehead. "I don't think I have a fever. But I ache all over. How do you feel, Asa?"

"I'm fine. Take care of the girls and yourself. If they fall asleep, you sleep too. I'll fix my supper when I'm done in the barn."

Adia looked at him with resignation and love. They'd known each other since their early teens. He hadn't changed from slim, strong, and handsome since their wedding day except to gain some gray hair. The outdoor work had aged his skin. His exposed skin seemed tough as her best leather satchel. From their intimacy she knew his body parts covered by clothes were like smooth pale alabaster.

Adia wondered why she could not tell him what she felt when he held her or she touched him. Asa had always been quiet when he reached for her in the night. Some people said loving words often, but neither Asa nor she expressed them.

Her eyes filled with tears as she thought of their girls. Prolonged illness was terrible and terrifying. The talk all over Worcester County was about quarantine against the new fever. People worried about an epidemic.

Was that the fever her girls had? Adia had prayed the girls would improve, but they hadn't. They were hot to the touch. Their sweet faces were flushed, and their foreheads had beads of perspiration constantly. Chills wracked their bodies. She tried to cool them and force them to drink water.

A doctor's visit would deplete their savings. Asa and she lived as carefully as they could. Adia twisted her hands together in worry. She looked at her hands, browned and strong. Calluses lined her palms from cleaning, sewing, and gardening. She couldn't just think about her life. The girls, she had to hurry upstairs and check on them.

Annelise, the most active early of the three children, had managed to climb out of her crib since early December, but not now. The older girls whimpered and seemed exhausted just moving to use the chamber pot. Ingelise talked enough to complain of a headache.

While picking up sewing work from her customers, Adia had heard of the constantly growing number of sick people. *Epidemic, polio, fevers, crippled for life* came to her ears. And word of mouth claimed this illness spread mostly to children. Could anyone guard against the sickness if they did not know what caused it?

If the sickness invaded a home, the household had to quarantine themselves for at least two weeks. Adia would not deliver the finished sewing to her customers for at least three weeks. The families would understand and be grateful she hadn't exposed them to the fever.

Adia squeezed fresh cloths with cool water in the porcelain bowl and then laid them on the girls' foreheads. As her hands hovered over them, she prayed, "Dear Lord, please help these little ones. They are in your care. We know you love them. Bring them through this, dear Lord. Help us to do everything we need to do for them."

"Thank you, Mama," Ingelise said in a raspy voice. Hanne just murmured and didn't open her eyes. Annelise didn't even murmur.

Adia gently ran her hands over her youngest child's little body. Annelise felt warmer than the others. She wore a simple flannel nightgown and a diaper. Although she had once tried using the chamber pot, imitating her big sisters, now she was a helpless baby. She hadn't said anything or seemed aware of her surroundings for a day.

Asa will have to fetch the doctor, Adia felt fear and tears as she offered the girls water. The older two sipped a cup, but Annelise barely opened her lips. Trying not to show her concern, Adia stayed with her girls, singing to them, changing the cloths, and offering water until she heard Asa enter the house.

Adia went to find Asa. She wanted to catch him quickly.In a minute she was in the mudroom with him. "Asa, you need to go for the doctor."

"Sure?"

"I'm sure. He's a good man, Asa. He will let us pay over time or give him some eggs or produce."

"I'll go." He looked at her a moment, caught his jacket and hat from pegs, and went to the barn for the horse.

Dr. Warren lived near the railroad station in Grafton. The land was a continuous range of hills, thickly wooded except where the land farmers had cleared and where the streams, rivers, and natural reservoirs ran. Asa knew Doctor Warren had a reputation as a fair, kind man. He would see their children as soon as possible even if Asa could give him no money today.

Doctor Warren agreed to come see the children immediately. He also rode a horse for this house call on this cold winter evening. Asa helped the doctor saddle the horse and led the way to the little house filled with sick children.

Asa and Adia stood behind the doctor as he examined the girls. The old Doctor who served native born and immigrants alike touched the sick children with gentleness and frowned with concern. The news he gave the concerned young parents frightened them. He left with words of encouragement, but they felt doubtful.

"Are you all right, Adia?" Asa asked later in their bedroom.

"Yes. You go to bed. You have to go to the mill early. But, are you sure you should go to work? The doctor was serious about quarantine."

"I have to go. We need the money even more now that . . ."

Asa lowered his head for a moment. When he did speak, his voice was hoarse with grief, and tears lay in his eyes. "They're so little, so helpless, Adia."

"God will help us all through this. You always remind us that God cares for us."

"He will. I know it. Sometimes I just . . . Work has been uneven. I'm sorry for that. I had high hopes you might not have to do so much work. I hoped I'd have enough to buy our own place by now. I nearly had enough. Paying the doctor, buying medicine, and the irregular work, we're set back."

"Asa, you take good care of us. We were fortunate to have this place. We'll be fine."

"Let's pray together," he suggested. They held hands.

They could see in the small bedroom under the eaves two of their feverish daughters in their bed, but Annelise, in the baby bed, was out of their sight.

Without closing their eyes or bowing their heads, they united in prayer. Asa prayed aloud. "Lord God, we know you love little children. We commit these girls and ourselves into your care. Help us to do our best for them and to trust you. Thank you for helping us through each day. We ask for your strength and healing power, and we ask this in Jesus' name. Amen."

Adia slumped against Asa. He let go of her hands and put his arms around her. "We'll get through this, Adia."

"I know. I know."

"Goodnight," he whispered and kissed her cheek, then her forehead, and finally her quivering lips.

Dawn's full light and chirping birds awoke Adia. She leaped to her feet and went to look at Annelise. The baby was fretful. Adia gave water and the medicine drops to Annelise. Then she turned to the other girls. They had kicked off their covers. Now they slept back-to-back. Their foreheads were no longer hot.

Adia signed with relief. Asa had left for work after he milked their cow. He would be so happy when he returned if the girls clearly felt better.

This morning, Adia fed them a nourishing broth and let them play and fall back to sleep. Annelise still tossed and turned with a fever. The doctor had said the worst time would have passed by today. Annelise whimpered pitifully. She hardly opened her eyes.

In the next few days, Ingelise and Hanne improved almost to full energy. Annelise continued to whimper, to have a fever, and difficulty swallowing. Her breathing was raspy. Whenever she was touched, she cried a miserable whimper of a sound, barely a kitten's mew.

The doctor's next visit found the family healthy, except Annelise. Her fever had finally broken, but she seemed weak and rarely moved. More distressing, she could not and did not move her right leg. Her right foot looked twisted, as if it had been wrenched inward, upward, toward her back. Nothing Adia tried helped the little foot to relax and straighten.

Polio. The doctor had said it softly on his first visit and clearly on his second. He could not explain why the two older girls only had the fever, headache, and sore throat. How was it possible that three children in the same house, in the same room, could be affected differently? The older girls fully recovered in seventy-two hours. Annelise had been ill over a week and now exhibited serious, probably life-long, complications.

Gently the doctor explained they should consider a move to Worcester to give Annelise the recommended therapy. He knew people who would buy their animals. Asa and Adia would simplify their household and give up the privacy of the small farm rental. Probably the best they would be able to find with the costs of medical care would be a triple-decker apartment.

For as long as Annelise's treatments were necessary, an apartment in a multi-storied house would be all they could afford. Asa would borrow or rent a wagon to move their belongings, especially the spinet piano, a gift for their fifth anniversary. He had said the gift was for both of them because Adia loved to play the piano. Asa wanted their home blessed with music. a house with a piano and music every day for their children. The purchase of the piano seemed silly to Adia now but Asa stubbornly disagreed.

He wouldn't sell the spinet unless they were desperate. He'd rather sleep and eat meals on the floor than sell their piano. Times would improve, he assured her. She could teach the children to play the piano. Asa said music soothed the soul and improved the mind.

Ingelise and Hanne were old enough to sense something was seriously wrong with Annelise. Adia had seen them looking at their baby sister with frowns. Ingelise seemed intent on keeping Hanne from going near Annelise.

Adia tried to promote sharing, but worry over the future distracted her They had lived in America long enough to have hope of a better future and to feel at home in Grafton, but now the hope and their plans had changed. Trusting one another and God stood as their foundation for the insecure future. Where would they end up in their new country?

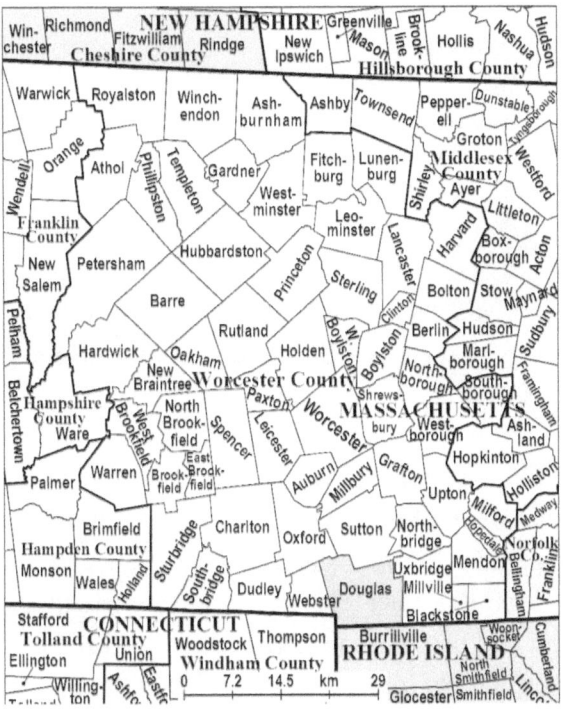

1940 Worcester County Map

2

DEFORMED

"Obvious breakages and deformities will affect the functional ability of the bird." **Danny Brown, *A Guide to Pigeons, Doves, and Quail***

I sat on the porch, watching my sisters run and play hopscotch and looked at my legs. Why couldn't I remember anything about the time when I had two healthy legs and feet? I looked at my small right leg, shrunken, and below it my twisted foot. Walking felt clumsy, and sometimes my hip and side hurt when I had to walk far.

When we lived in Worcester, I sat on the porch often. My two older sisters attended school, and my parents left for their jobs while the elderly neighbor watched over me. I felt alone because she took frequent naps.

Worcester triple-decker houses early 20th century

Six immigrant families lived in our three-floor apartment building. We were the only Danish family and the smallest family. Others in the building were two Armenian families, each with four children and grandparents, an Italian family with five children, and two Irish families, one with five children, the other with eight. Even though lots of children lived around us, they didn't play with me. They ran, climbed, skipped, tumbled, hopped, and jumped-rope.

Our apartment was the smallest. Mama said Papa told us we needed to save every penny to buy land, a house and farm. My parents didn't want to live in the city forever.

I couldn't play with friends who easily ran up and down the stairs in our triple-decker. Because I couldn't play their games or do chores with my sisters and other children in the building, I longed to feel that they missed me and wanted to include me. Really, I knew my sisters were happier without me. Ingelise ignored me more completely than Hanne did.

Papa and Mama didn't notice because they worked long hours every day. They had to pay bills—my medical bills—

and save for the farm. Our family talk in evenings often focused on our future farm. Mama and Papa described the farm so well, I could picture it.

I asked where our new farm was and everyone laughed. *Nearby*, Papa said. Then he smiled at Mama and my sisters as if they knew something I didn't. Sometimes Hanne looked at me like she did not understand my words. Ingelise looked at me like I was stupid.

Papa worked three jobs that I knew about, and he repaired items at home late into the evenings. I wished he could have fixed my foot and leg as easily as he repaired bicycles and wagons. He was handy with anything. One time he worked in Fitchburg making bicycles. He'd been a machinist there. Mama said he felt glad when he got a job as a Worcester machinist.

Ingelise seemed grouchy when she talked to me or even when she looked at me. Hanne stayed quiet and near Ingelise. Perhaps they were angry because I could read? Mama read to me many times during the day, ten minutes here, 15 minutes there. I loved to hear her read, but I hadn't started school, so I asked Mama to teach me. Mama taught me slowly but I loved it so I practiced. Sometimes Hanne asked about the books I read, but Ingelise never did.

Mama cleaned homes and did sewing and laundry for rich families but not every day. When she was home, she read to me, showed me other skills and drills to develop my piano playing. Often her employers let her bring books to read to us. Sometimes they gave her the books or their children's outgrown clothes. I enjoyed the books hour after hour, but oh, how I longed to walk into a store that sold clothes as fine as the hand-me-downs Mama brought home! We wished for lives like the children with the fine blouses, skirts, dressed, tights, slips, and shoes.

When I grew up, I wanted to wear fine clothes. I would have to get a good job to afford lovely clothes. Could I do that? I told myself I would.

The beautiful books and clothes made me wish to see the houses and children who owned these. Ingelise and Hanne had seen some of those houses. They had accompanied Mama or Papa on errands into those neighborhoods. Ingelise and Hanne talked about the houses, the yards, the carriage houses, the playhouses, the porches, and the flowerbeds. They enjoyed talking about all they had seen. I felt like they wanted me to know I had been excluded from something they enjoyed with Mama.

I had already learned children in my neighborhood could be mean, but it was strange my sisters were among that group. Little children asked me questions about why I walked funny, not intending to be mean. I wondered if everyone physically different felt this isolation from others even some family members.

When I went somewhere, since I could not run and climb, I sat still and noticed details. And since I could talk a lot faster than I could walk, I asked many questions. Mama joked and asked me how I could breathe when I said so much so fast. Papa said I should stop talking long enough for his brain to catch up to my questions.

These comments about my talking were just jokes, but I worried about making Mama and Papa tired. Every day they worked hard. My problems as a cripple complicated their lives.

I wanted them to feel proud of me. Stuck in the apartment so much, I kept thinking I should work on being smart. Numbers seemed like a game to me, so I did math for fun. I asked my sisters questions about their lessons. They gave me brief answers. I asked neighbor children about their school work. They showed me their lessons glad for any help or ideas.

Mama said she loved to see me learn so I asked her to teach me the piano. I felt sure we had the most wonderful mother in the world. She worked hard each day for us and helped neighbors. If I developed talent for the piano, I might always have a special place in her heart.

I worried that she and Papa might grow tired of me, like Ingelise and Hanne had. So, I practiced the piano. I loved to play songs and scales. Mama said she didn't know any six-year-old who played as well as I did. I played by ear the songs we sang as a family or the ones Mama sang to us.

On winter evenings, Mama gave all us girls piano lessons. We sat on the piano bench while she instructed us. My sisters didn't take to the piano.

"Mama, this is as difficult as homework," Ingelise complained.

"My fingers are stiff." Hanne kept repeating.

"I'm tired of sitting straight, Mama" Ingelise continued.

"Please, Mama, can we be done?" Hanne would beg.

I loved my turn sitting next to Mama on the piano bench and the feel of the keys beneath my fingertips. Creating music made me feel powerful. I couldn't manage the pedals for many years, and when I did, only with my good foot. I loved every opportunity to play for Mama or Papa or neighbors who stopped in. People in our building told Mama they liked to hear the songs she played. Mama beamed when she told them the piano player was her youngest daughter. Then those people stared more at me with a glimmer of interest.

When my sisters left for school, I stayed in the apartment. I could work without interruption. Being alone did not frighten me. I played the piano, read, and created songs, but I didn't know how to write. I memorized the songs without the written words and music.

Dozens of days with awful weather didn't allow me to walk on the icy porch, steps, and sidewalks. My corrective shoe and brace made it difficult to move over slippery surfaces. Mama and Papa had purchased a wide assortment of equipment doctors suggested, though nothing worked well. My right foot was twisted in an odd, sideways position and was smaller and weak. I exercised, but nothing strengthened my leg. Mama and Papa always looked for new equipment or therapies, but nothing straightened my leg or strengthened my muscles.

Working on home projects could fill my day. I talked to any neighbor within calling distance. They all knew my name, though many called me Ann or Anna.

Because of my leg and foot, it took too long for me to go downstairs and outside to the outhouse. One cold windy day Ingelise came back inside with the empty porcelain chamber pot and whispered to me, "Work on your exercises. Taking care of you is hard on us all. Do you know that? If you don't work on getting stronger, you are selfish or stupid."

On the days that Mama cleaned for families on Salisbury, Elm, Park, and Highland Streets, she arrived home late. She'd have some neighbor listen for my call, and if no trustworthy neighbor was available, Ingelise had to stay with me—against her wishes. The way she talked to me, even the way she moved around me showed her irritation.

The triple-decker houses had a porch on each level. The porches did not wrap around the building, but were small floor spaces with a railing and a roof above. Worcester had only a few weeks of summer's hot and muggy weather. In the summer families moved beds onto the porches to sleep.

I would have started first grade in Worcester but Mama said we would move. Mama seemed sad, but she said she did not feel sad, just tired. She didn't clean houses for wealthy families as much, and did less washing and sewing. Ingelise and Hanne helped more than they had, but it seemed odd to see Mama's energy and spirit so low, especially when Papa had found a house and land he could buy.

In late summer of 1909, Papa put every saved penny as a down payment on a small farm near the town of Holden. He looked like a man who had just won a lottery and wanted us to feel happy about moving to Holden. He told us every fact he learned about the town. Once, John Hancock, a Massachusetts governor, donated Holden's town green and the land for a Meeting House in the hopes of winning the support of the community before an election.

One night I heard Papa telling Mama some of the stories about Holden that had scary history. I wondered about ghosts of people who had died violently. The Nipmuc Indian Wars took place with settlers. The fighting was fierce and frightening.

One day, Papa told us at dinner that he had settled the moving details so we could leave the triple-decker in Worcester for our own farm in Holden by the end of the summer. Bringing the stew to the table, Mama stood still with her mouth open, too stunned to speak. She stared at his face for a minute and then smiled. It was a smile like the sun coming out on a cloudy day.

"When will we move?" she asked as she set the pot on the table.

"Day after tomorrow," Papa said. He looked around at us as if to say, *start getting ready*. We were ready. After our family devotions, filled with prayers of thanksgiving, we started packing. Mama looked more energetic than she had in a while. I wondered if gaining weight caused her to be so tired. She certainly had gotten thicker over the summer.

I could hardly sleep that night. I wiggled so much Ingelise and Hanne threatened I would sleep on the floor if I didn't stay still, but they were excited, too. The dream would come true! Papa said so, and I believed him.

3

DEPENDING ON A DREAM

"Doves can be lively backyard inhabitants, and many birders enjoy the company of both fledglings and adults exploring their surroundings. By providing the most reliable wooden bird houses, any birder can attract doves and their families to become regular guests." **Bird Watching Academy**

On moving day much earlier than usual, everyone in the family carried something to the large rented wagon and our small wagon. Even I carried a few things on my one trip to the wagon. Then Papa told me to wait in the wagon while everything else was packed.

Neighbor men helped carry heavy furniture, like the piano, before they left for work. Papa tried to pay them, but they refused money. He had helped them with repairs, and Mama had made soup and meals for neighbors when their money was low or their families were sick. They knew the Bible verse about doing unto others what you would want others to do unto you. My parents lived by that verse. With everyone pitching in, the apartment was soon empty.

Papa took his place on the driver's seat after Mama, Inge-lise, and I were set in the new little wagon not brand new, but it was new to us. Papa said a second wagon would help in his work. He could use the best one for the job, or he might hire a day laborer to help him with a big job. Worcester always had people who needed work.

We felt excited sitting on the big satchels with our belongings. They were stacked behind the driver's seat. Papa and Hanne led the way as he drove the big rented wagon. That was the only time Hanne was happy away from Inge-lise. My heart felt caught in a whirlwind. We were on our way to a new life.

One pause occurred before we moved forward in the wagons. Papa prayed in Danish. Before his *amen,* Mama said a prayer in English, "Thank you, dear Lord, for your help and care. Protect us on this journey to our new home. Help us realize all we have comes from you. Bless and guide us each day and help us to live for you." She said her *amen* in English and our *amens* followed.

Papa said *giddyup* to the big dray that pulled the rented wagon, and Mama made a clucking sound to our horse, Berde. Berde means *glacier* in Danish. Berde was a tall, light-gray gelding and a good work horse, but I had also heard Papa talk about getting a younger horse that could pull a small cart.

We left the city of Worcester and the triple-decker on a steep hill for the farm Papa had purchased in Holden, six miles away. Our farm was located on Bailey Road. On our trip we passed other riders and wagons, people on bicycles, and people in carriages of various sizes. Some smiled at us.

Some ignored us, and some just stared like we were a new type of creature.

Holden, in 1909, seemed a good-sized town. The Worcester Consolidated Railway Line gave the Holden residents a connection to Worcester, Boston, and beyond. We crossed the railroad tracks to Bailey Road, and we continued up and down the hills gentle in size compared to the steep hills of Worcester.

Bailey Road looked muddy. After we passed the railroad tracks, the wagons almost got stuck, but the big work horse pulled out of the sucking mire and so did our dear Berde. Soon Papa waved back and told us it was the last hill. The road formed a Y; Papa pointed to the left. A house beyond the Y faced us as if it waited for us to arrive.

There's our house, our barn, our farm. Tingles and shivers ran through my spine. *This is our special place.* I felt sure of it.

We drove the wagons between the house and the barn. The house looked as long on the side as it was broad in the front. Papa jumped down and lifted Hanne down, then Ingelise. I stayed where I was seated. My sisters didn't move because Papa said, "I want to walk Mama to the house first," He helped Mama from the small wagon.

They walked slowly toward the house, arm in arm. Ingelise and Hanne moved to have a better view. We all noticed the special way Mama and Papa stared at each other. They paused and hugged. It was rare we saw them hug one another.

Then Ingelise turned to Hanne and me and said, "Our new farmhouse and barn are literally on the other side of the tracks. Did you notice that?"

I turned and asked, "Why does it matter that we crossed the railroad tracks?"

Ingelise glared and explained, careful not to say it loudly.

"When people are far out of town and cross the railroad tracks, that means they are in the poor side of town."

Ingelise told us that we were in the poor side of town in front of our new house, before we enjoyed anything. My chest hurt. Ingelise had a sour spirit. I didn't know why.

Our parents were among the best and kindest parents, but Ingelise didn't ever act as though she thought we had good parents or a decent life. Hanne looked from our happy parents, to me, to Ingelise, and said nothing. I turned to look at Mama and Papa.

The farm made Papa and Mama happy, so I loved it. Often when I had been alone at home in Worcester, I wondered if I would ever live on my own. If I never got strong enough to a house, job, or husband of my own, at least I could live on this farm with Mama and Papa.

Mama smiled as she walked up the porch steps to the front door beside Papa. She touched the house's outer wall. The house had white clapboards with a large chimney on each side. Stones starting from huge to smaller made the chimneys.

The house's broad front included four windows below and four above. That number of windows seemed luxurious. The first-floor windows contained little panes and looked so clean they sparkled. Three stone steps led to the wide front door.

"Here we are, Adia, our new home, our own farm," Papa said clear enough for us to hear the happiness in his voice.

"God be praised," Mama answered and turned right there by the front door, stood up on her tiptoes, and gave Papa a kiss on his lips.

Ingelise rolled her eyes. Hanne wide-eyed looked at me to see if I saw the kiss. I laughed at her expression.

Papa smiled too as he turned to us. "Come along, girls."

Ingelise and Hanne ran to the porch.

"Wait, girls. I want us to go in together," he said.

Mama and my sisters stood still. Papa came to the wagon. I leaned over the seat so he could easily lift me, but he didn't put me down.

"Let's go around to the back porch and go in that way. You can see the space where we can have a vegetable garden, and this land has fruit trees and blackberry bushes. There's a pump above a well in the backyard too."

Papa carried me around the house and we saw a stone-based back porch. It had a few steps up to a dutch door and frames for windows, but what covered the window space didn't look like glass. Mama, Ingelise, and Hanne followed Papa up onto that porch after he opened the door. I reached out and touched one of the windows.

"What is it Papa? It's not glass."

"Eisenglass, made from earth minerals."

"Almost clear."

"Yes. Look out now at the land, Annelise." I did. The land that seemed to stretch far back to a thick line of woods.

Papa stood me up on the porch and reached to take Mama's hands. He opened the dark oak door into the house, he kept holding hands with Mama. Ingelise, Hanne and I followed.

"This is a work room," Papa proclaimed.

"At the big houses in Worcester, the ladies call this their mud room," Mama replied.

"Why is it a mud room?" Ingelise asked.

"People coming into the house can leave dirty shoes and boots in this room. People bringing in something like fresh cut flowers or vegetables can wash off dirt in this room."

Then Papa led us into the kitchen. A closet stood across from the doorway. Next to the closet I saw a huge metal box in front of a black iron stove. The box seemed filled it with stacks of different sized wood.

The black iron stove looked capable of giving us more heat than the stove we had in the apartment. A full row of cupboards was on the right wall. Beyond them was counter of slate, and an inside pump right by and black stone sink. Mama looked happy but also had tears in her eyes.

"This is a lovely kitchen, Asa," Mama declared and smiled at Papa.

"Come this way into the dining room," Papa's voice had the happiness that glowed in Mama's face. He led us into the dining room. Across the room stood a built-in corner China closet. To the left was a fireplace. To the right we saw stairs and beneath the stairs a door stood open revealing storage room.

Ingelise's and Hanne's eyes glowed with excitement as they turned toward the stairs. They did a little dance, waiting for Papa to tell them they could go up the stairs. Ingelise frowned when Papa motioned for them to follow him and he led us to the front of the house. If we had come in the front door, we would have seen an open space, a hall way and off to the right side beyond the front door, another room.

Mama walked forward into that big room. "A parlor!" Mama exclaimed.

We moved into the big square of a room with three windows, one to the east, and two on the south side. All the windows in the main house had real glass. Sunlight streaming in those windows made the empty room seemed fancy.

"If that's what you want it to be," Papa commented.

"What else could it be? The piano will fit in here so well! We won't seem crowded at all." Mama seemed amazed and delighted.

I didn't know what a parlor was. Hanne and Ingelise weren't interested. They wandered back to stand near the stairs.

"All right, you two. Race up those stairs." Papa freed them with his words. Mama walked, and Papa carried me upstairs.

At the top left was a small room. To the right was a large one. A doorway between the two rooms showed a few stairs into an attic.

"Go on up," he said and Ingelise, Hanne, and Mama were up those stairs in moments. Papa carried me again. I could go up and down stairs but slowly. He set me near a window. I looked on the porch roof and the backyard.

"So much space, Asa," Mama said with a great sigh. She went down the stairs and returned to the larger bedroom. Ingelise and Hanne followed, and Papa helped me down the steps. I watched from the attic doorway. Ingelise and Hanne took another look out the bedroom window in the small bedroom that would be ours. Then they fluttered through the house like moths.

Papa and Mama stood near one another. He gazed around him and finally back at me. I leaned against the door jamb.

"Time to unload the wagon," was all he said before he swooped me up and carried me down the stairs and onto the porch. "You'll enjoy the fresh air here while we bring things inside," Papa said as he put me down.

I leaned against the wooden porch wall and held onto one of the front porch columns. They did not seem wide, not majestic like the houses of the rich in Worcester, but they looked clean, straight, and strong. I thought about those qualities and wished I had them.

Through the rest of the daylight hours, we unpacked and arranged rugs, furniture, and additional household items. It seemed moving in was much easier than I had imagined, but I understood that was because Papa had worked hard to prepare the new house. Two men Papa had hired showed up to carry in the heaviest pieces of furniture, including the piano.

As we moved in our belongings, we realized Papa had cleaned the farmhouse to Mama's high standards: floors, windows, and walls. He had done this as a gift, so on moving day we could put away everything and settle in without having to clean. *When did he find the time to do this?*

I knew then how much he loved our mother. Papa was always working for us all, but especially for Mama. He wanted her happy in the new home. If she was happy, we would have a good home. I could not imagine any reason would rise to destroy her happiness in this wonderful little farm of ours.

4

NOT INTERCHANGEABLE

"... the difference between a pigeon and a dove, a pigeon is a member of the family Columbiformes. A pigeon may technically be of any size. Aviculturists and naturalists have arbitrarily divided these birds into two groups based on a relative body size. This essentially means that a dove is a small pigeon, and consequently a pigeon is a large dove. Their names are therefore interchangeable ..." **Danny Brown, *A Guide to Pigeons, Doves, and Quail***

Our farmhouse dated back to the early 1800s. Even though the house looked good on the outside and was clean on the inside, Papa had to do many repairs: roof leaks, worm-rotted boards, crumbling foundation corners, and the edge of the well. He fixed them all, cared for the farm. Papa also worked at a new machinist job in Worcester, and assigned chores so we all participated in running the farm.

Most of my chores I could do while sitting, but I also checked the chicken roosts for eggs each day. Sometimes I pulled weeds in the vegetable patches closest to the house. If the eggs needed collecting immediately, Ingelise or Hanne gathered them. I collected the eggs well if I didn't rush. If I rushed, I was clumsy.

I liked having chores, but I didn't like to watch Ingelise and Hanne work quickly around me and past me. I had learned the foolishness of trying to match their pace. Mama never spoke about my lack of speed or my clumsiness. She was strict in what she expected of us, but always made me feel better, calmer, and happier.

Pregnant with a fourth child in our first fall in our new home, Mama still managed to add autumn flowers and herb beds. Weeding was a task I could do sitting or kneeling. I loved the smell of the flowers and herbs. I felt freer outside, even if I walked lopsided as a stringed puppet with an inexperienced puppeteer. I wished I would walk evenly one day.

Papa used his level to build things straight and even. I watched him and wished he could level me. I longed to move without depending on a person, cane, or horse. The freedom to move easily and smoothly would be a miracle.

I told Mama about my desires, and she said I had moved smoothly before the polio. Infantile paralysis was the fancy big name for the sickness I had. Mama told me that I had been strong and active, walking and crawling earlier than either Ingelise or Hanne. In my dreams I still ran as well as they did. While I might not move easily again, Mama assured me God would have new ways for me to develop strength.

We made friends with the neighbors on Bailey Road. Mrs. Vandervort, a Dutch woman seemed to have a kind heart but she hardly ever had a talk with Mama or us without giving instructions. She was tall, skinny, square, and even had muscles anyone could see when she lifted something heavy. I thought she was almost as strong and capable as my father.

She and her husband had six children—three boys and three girls—and they had a farm closer to the railroad tracks and town. She organized and improved everything within her reach. I couldn't decide if she might be a strict fairy godmother or a business-like witch.

As Mama's birthing time neared, Mrs. Vandervort volunteered to help. She had delivered her own children and helped many other women. Mrs. Vandervort told us the birth went smoothly. The new family member—another girl—was born on February 26, 1910.

Mrs. Vandervort called Papa upstairs. We girls waited in the kitchen. I heard Mrs. Vandervort tell my father it had been a short labor. Mother and child were doing well and as usual she gave instructions. "Go and have some time with your wife and new daughter," Mrs. Vandervort told Papa.

Mama and Papa named our new sister, Ebba, which meant *strength*. Ebba had a strong cry when she entered the world. Papa and I heard Ebba's first cry. Ingelise and Hanne talked to each other, so they missed it.

While Papa saw Mama and Ebba, Mrs. Vandervort instructed us older sisters to be kind and gentle with the new baby. She said the baby would look up to us and trust us, and we were to take that trust as a holy responsibility from God. Physically, babies were delicate, and they had to be handled carefully and kept out of drafts. We should see that Mama didn't work hard while she was nursing the baby. We should help as much as we could.

Mrs. Vandervort had us each practice holding a ten-pound sack of flour. It stood for the baby. I asked how heavy our baby sister really was, and Mrs. Vandervort said Ebba was half as heavy as the sack. With an expression on her face as sturdy as a wooden shoe, Mrs. Vandervort adjusted our hold on the sack and gave us directions about touching the top of the baby's head. All babies had a soft spot for about six months. I was amazed at that fact, but Ingelise or Hanne just looked relieved when Mrs. Vandervort turned her attention to fixing dinner.

Mrs. Vandervort made a wonderful dinner, left it simmering on the stove, and returned to her home to fix her own family their dinner. She had done chores early that morning for her own household. Mama and Papa spoke about Mrs. Vandervort as a gift from the Lord. Once Mama called her an angel. That made me look at Mrs. Vandervort differently, and it also caused me to wonder about angels. I read all the Bible stories about angels that I could find and I knew angels had different purposes. Sometimes angels looked just like a regular person, but sometimes they appeared dazzling. I never read about one that looked like a crippled person, but I guessed that could happen and would even be a good disguise.

Papa called us to see our new sister, the older girls ran past me. I pulled myself up along the banisters or sat on a step, pushed myself by my arms one step at a time thinking about my new baby sister. Ebba, I felt she would be the most special person in my life. I doubted Ingelise or Hanne felt that because I had heard them talking about how much harder life would be for Mama and Papa with four children. Ingelise didn't seem to like babies, and Hanne followed Ingelise in almost everything.

I stood well enough when the blur of my sisters, laughing and giggling, pushed past me leaving the room. Just a minute with Mama, Papa and our new sister seemed enough for them. I arrived at the foot of the bed. Papa moved to stand near me.

Mama looked happy, tired, but pretty in a night gown I hadn't seen. Yellow with tiny flowers, the gown had a ruffle at the neck and buttons leading down under the covers. Dark shadows—purple sickle moons under her eyes and on either side of her nose.

Papa lifted me onto the double bed near Mama's. Ingelise and Hanne returned to watch me meet Ebba. What did they think I would do?

"This is Ebba," Mama said with the baby in the crook of her arm.

Papa took the baby and let me hold her for a minute. Ebba was much lighter than the flour sack. She looked like a tiny, bald old person. But oh my! Did she smell fresh! Ebba smelled wonderful!

Ebba yawned while I held her, and I had my face close to her tiny mouth when it was stretched wide. I loved the innocent scent of her baby skin and breath. I felt her muscles moving as she wiggled and gave a tiny shiver. Tiny, but she had the name of *strength*.

"She is so tiny." I exclaimed.

"Oh, she'll grow," Mama assured us.

"But we'll always be bigger. Older, I mean," Ingelise declared in a bossy tone.

"That's right. And you big sisters will be good examples. God wants us to be good examples in our family and to other people. Let's pray together."

Papa nodded and had us hold hands. He launched into a prayer committing our new baby and us to do the Lord's work and will each day. I prayed along but with my own request. Please, dear God, let me be special to Ebba. Don't let her just see the older sisters as interchangeable. Help me to love her best and to be her favorite. Please. Amen.

I THOUGHT I could be the big sister who knew the most. Ebba would look up to Ingelise and Hanne for many things, but I wanted her to think I was the smartest and the most attentive of her big sisters. Maybe she could even think it was fun to spend time with me. I could read with expression to Ebba like Mama read to me.

I looked in the family Bible for important dates and then asked Mama for more details about our family. She and Papa had been married in the spring of 1896 in a typical Danish, farm-community wedding. An arch of pine branches had been built outside her home doorway for them to walk beneath as a married couple, a Danish tradition.

The other tradition was to serve a marzipan cake, sometimes called a cornucopia cake. It was very sweet and filled with fruit. They cut the cake with each other's hand on the knife and then fed each guest a piece. Because Mama's father had died, the entire wedding party made a trip to the cemetery, and she placed her bouquet on her father's grave.

Mama's wedding dress was dark bottle green of light weight wool. The dress was practical and plain and of the best quality fabric. She would use it for dressy occasions for years. As a bride, she wore her hair braided with a special arrangement of flowers and ribbons as a head band. Mama still had her wedding dress. She put on the dress one day when Ingelise and Hanne were at school. Mama laughed at how snug it felt, but she could wear it.

I was proud of my mother's beauty, abilities, and temperament. Papa had been a smart man to pick her. Mama seemed just as happy with her choice of a husband.

Mama and Papa had an adventurous streak in their spirits. A few months after their wedding, Papa left for America. He was one of over twenty thousand people to leave

Denmark between 1870 and 1900. Papa had many building and mechanical skills.

He found a job quickly. Letters from him and friends who had immigrated to America gave Mama hope they would soon be reunited. When he had earned the money, Papa sent for Mama. Though I often tried to imagine their time apart, it was beyond my imagination.

By the time Papa sent for Mama, over a year had passed. They lived in Fitchburg at first. Ingelise was born there in 1899. Hanne followed by arriving in April of 1901. Mama called them her turn-of-the-century babies. Grafton was my birthplace in August of 1905, three months after my parents rented the small farm where Grafton touched the edge of Worcester.

Now, Ebba arrived in 1910. Holden felt like our best home to me. I wondered if Mama and Papa would have any more children. Girls, they only had daughters. Did they want a son? I didn't ever ask *that* question.

Now, I could have started at the Dawson Elementary School with my sisters, but Mama and Papa did not think I could physically handle the school trip and a school day. I wondered if their fears were based on not embarrassing Ingelise and Hanne because they knew my big sisters did not like having a crippled sister.

Mama taught me all she could. I listened and practiced. I wanted to learn the subjects Ingelise and Hanne studied. Mama admitted teaching me helped her grow in her use of English. Daily, together we practiced writing English. She had beautiful handwriting so I copied it as best I could.

We had an old set of McGuffey readers—real old. Papa said they were from before the Civil War. Papa had gathered the set of eight books from the garbage pile of a wealthy people in Worcester. With these books, Mama and I wrote the alphabet, learned lessons about families, animals, and the world, practiced reading about patriotism, honesty, charity, thrift, hard work, courage, reverence, respect, spelling, poetry, nature, fables, grammar, and arithmetic. After a year in Holden, Mama and I had worked through four books.

Mama only gave me small bits at a time, but told me I could do more if I wanted to. And I always did. Sometimes when Ingelise and Hanne talked about their school lessons, Mama would look at me as if to say, *don't you want to say something?* I smiled and kept what I knew to myself. My instinct warning me not to make Ingelise and Hanne aware of my knowledge. They would be miserable to me if I could read and write. Mama must have agreed because she didn't tell them about what I was learning either.

5

PUDGE, LOCAL POWERS, AND SCHOOL

"While shy and friendly, doves lead in their own way, usually quietly and ever so consciously. Sure, doves are submissive and indecisive, they're the builders (and backbones) of relationships and communities. Quietly stubborn, doves are known to dig their heels into the sand. Sometimes stubborn, other times accommodating. In the end, doves are likely to say: "let's have harmony and keep the peace." **Tick-dove-personality type**

Over all her years in Massachusetts, Mama cleaned big houses twice a week for two wealthy families with children. Those jobs provided us with many cast-off clothes. Usually, Ingelise used the clothes first or had first choice. Hanne got the hand-me-downs, then they came to me. Our clothing was well- worn, but beautiful, far nicer than we could ever buy. The clothes were all wonderful fabrics, colors, warm, and soft.

Mama also sewed or repaired clothing for pay. At home, she cleaned, washed, ironed, sewed, and did the farm work.

Somehow, she stayed cheerful. Mama enjoyed gardening, teaching me, caring for Ebba, cooking, baking, and making us feel loved.

When I held little Ebba, I told her Bible stories, fairytales, and stories about our family. I wasn't sure when or if I would have my own friends, so I invested more love and attention in Ebba. She could be my friend and sister. Mama always looked happy when she saw me enjoying time with Ebba. Ingelise and Hanne spent their time at home talking, playing, and working together without showing any special interest in me or Ebba.

Papa earned two dollars a week for his factory job. Two dollars didn't seem like much, but wages were similar in the different factories. Papa did many side jobs too. He and Mama tithed, bought necessities, applied the largest portion to paying off our property, and saved the rest against an unknown disaster or necessary project. No frivolous spending.

To Papa, property ownership grew roots in his new country, and provided a solid foundation for the family's future. He purchased acres tucked off the main road, route 122A, which ran east to west through Holden. A pond and a stream lay on the property. Our Bailey Road connected 122A to the long road that ran beside Reservoir Road.

Worcester wanted more water from the Holden Reservoir, even though the city had other water sources. Papa thought the town fathers unwise to sell water rights. He said they lacked foresight and imagination. Hearing the word *imagination* from my father made me wonder what he had imagined for his dream of a farm. I felt sure a crippled child was not a part of his dream, but he made me feel like he loved me as much as the other girls.

When I looked at Ebba, I remembered Ingelise had said

everything would be different if the new baby were a boy. She said all men wanted at least one son. Ingelise said if we got a brother, we'd see Papa treat him special.

I didn't agree with Ingelise. If Papa was disappointed in having another daughter when Ebba arrived, he didn't show those feelings. I always felt Papa loved us, even when he was scolding us.

I PROBABLY WAS the laziest person in our house because no one demanded I hurry. My family and others waited for me —a girl with an uneven and gimpy leg—to accomplish my tasks. My parents made allowances that I could choose how to spend time inside the house while my sisters worked outside or ran up and down stairs, carrying things for cleaning, storing, or rearranging. Even for outside chores, I didn't have to exert myself. I wasn't tall, and I started to get chubby.

I don't apply the word *chubby to* myself. I had heard Ingelise call others *chubby.* One day Papa felt playful. He picked us up one by one, threw us in the air, not high enough to frighten us, but enough to make us squeal or laugh, and caught us.

After he caught me, he teased, "Annelise, I believe you have a bit of pudge. Did you take Ebba's baby fat?"

Ingelise and Hanne laughed a lot at that comment. Pudge, chub, fat. Ebba giggled. Mama was inside. I frowned when Papa put me down.

He asked, "Now where's that smile?" which *could* have made me smile again, except he added one word, "Now where's that smile, Pudge?"

Pudge. I hated it. I looked at Ingelise, Hanne, and Ebba, and saw they had no extra roundness. Like Papa and Mama, they were sparse and browned from their outside activities. I alone had pudge and paleness. My pudge betrayed the amount of time I spent sitting rather than running.

I trudged back to the house, trying my hardest not to walk with the extreme seesaw gait that marked me as a cripple. In a way I wished Mama had heard Papa's comment. She would have realized I hated a nickname like Pudge! I hoped Papa wouldn't say it again in front of Ingelise and Hanne. They might start using it! I was horrified to think I might hear the word from Ebba's mouth one day.

Once I was inside the house, Mama asked me to set the table for dinner. The kitchen was warm though the outside air contained a cold autumn tingle. The smell of chicken potpie and home-baked bread made my mouth water. Mama could make a great meal in quick time. If a neighbor had health problems or someone from our church family was sick, Mama cooked or baked something and took it to them.

She had a chance to practice this generosity with the church we had attended since we moved to Holden. Many people in the church took food or clothes to help people in need. We joined the Holden First Baptist Church in 1909. The Church family was a mixture of Swedish, Danish, Canadian, Polish, Russian, Italian, and British families. Mama and Papa liked this. They found a common bond of people from many countries. No one made me feel uncomfortable by stares, even though I was the only crippled person in the congregation.

People said Baptists had been in town since the Revolutionary War days, but for years they had to meet in the Tavern on Route 31 or traveled together sometimes to meet with Baptists in the Templeton Baptist Church. They wanted to build their own church building but the town fathers, who were all members of the Congregational Church, denied the Baptists' petition to build a church.

"Mama, how could the Congregational members stop other churches from coming into town?" I asked as I learned more about the church history.

"Your father told me that the Congregational church was like the state church until years after the Revolutionary War. They even had any groups in town pay them some of the tax money, poll parish taxes your Papa told me. People just didn't stand up against this control until almost forty years after the United States was a country."

"That's a long time!"

"Yes, but you will see that standing up and speaking out against unfairness is hard. I pray for you and your sisters to be fair, kind, and to have courage."

FINALLY, Mama and Papa let me, at age nine, attend the Dawson school in 1914. Mama had taught me all she could. They knew I should face the world with its daily challenges and put aside dreams of walking normally. Even if other children were mean, I needed to learn how to be out in the world more and in school days I could mostly stay seated.

I remained patient when Papa called me *Pudge*. It wasn't often. Ingelise called me *Slow Poke,* and I preferred that to Pudge. I tried to erase the nicknames from my mind, but they lodged in my heart. And the heart is difficult place to heal.

Although I tried to be kind to my older sisters, Ingelise got angry if I helped her with school work. Mama heard Ingelise say, "Don't try to help me. You don't go to school."

Not long after those comments, Mama enrolled me in

Dawson School, a one-room schoolhouse. Holden had eleven school buildings. Each school functioned separately and was represented by one man on the central school committee.

From our farm, the trip was L-shaped. We walked the foot of the L south on Bailey Road, then turned right and walked the long stem of the L northeast to the school. The road was curvy like most area roads. Papa said, "Settlers made roads over old Indian paths. Indians have a different attitude toward the earth from most white people."

When we could ride on the school wagon, I felt shivers of happiness. How excited I was to sit aboard the children's school wagon! Ingelise and Hanne helped me into it quickly. Most children on the wagon were acquaintances, so no one stared at my foot and leg.

My first day at the Dawson School, I noticed Ingelise had the nicest and newest outfit of our family, but her shoes looked worn out. Hanne's shoes weren't any better. I wondered if this difference was another reason why we weren't close. Maybe they thought about the cost of my shoes and braces and it meant they couldn't have new shoes.

That first day, my nervousness went beyond the emotional pain of Ingelise and Hanne's attitudes. The building was a large clapboard square with a roof-covered porch, facing Salisbury Road. Not everything about Dawson suited me. Two outhouses—boys' and girls'—were at the back far side at the edge of the woods. I hadn't given that a thought. I hoped I never had to use it more than once a day because my limp would take me a while. If I went during lunch, I wouldn't miss school lessons or time with the teacher.

Dawson one room school house was destroyed by fire in the fall of 1926.

Mr. Foster, who drove the school wagon, stopped the horses near the front porch, on which a pretty woman, our young teacher, stood greeting us with cheerful words and a smile. Why hadn't Ingelise or Hanne mentioned how beautiful the teacher was? Why hadn't they told us that she had a voice like sunshine and words like a rainbow? She wore glasses, had her auburn hair pulled back tightly from her oval face, and showed a warm smile. Her clothes were a plain white shirt with buttons and a dark-blue wool skirt. She looked like her name, Miss MacIntosh. She was one of the first female teachers in the town of Holden.

I clumped my way to the steps to the porch alone; Ingelise and Hanne never waited for me. Mama and Papa didn't want me to expect special help and consideration. They hoped my older sisters would show more care for me, but if they didn't, Mama and Papa wanted me to do my best.

Miss MacIntosh touched my shoulder gently as she said good morning each day. I'd seen her touch others' shoulders so she hadn't done the kind act because I was a cripple. In the large room that was our classroom, everyone sat according to age. The front row was for new and very young students.

Hanne sat in the third row; Ingelise in the back. On the cool September morning, everyone kept on her or his sweaters. No fire burned in the stove. Ingelise told me the oldest boys brought the wood in, but the teacher made the fire when we needed it. Bright sunlight streamed in the eastern windows. I sat in a seat in the sunlight.

Miss MacIntosh walked to the front, welcomed us, and gave a speech about believing we would have a good year. She could tell we wanted to make our families proud. She had high hopes we would all learn a lot. Then she went over basic procedures and rules.

She had been last year's replacement, and most students and their parents thought she worked hard, was fair, and encouraged the students. I liked her from the time I first saw her, and not because she was my first teacher. I'd always count Mama as that. I remember glancing back at the rows of older students. I wondered if my sisters had known how to read and write and to do simple problems before they started school.

Mama cautioned us against being opinionated. We shouldn't judge people by how they looked, spoke, or acted. Jesus was the only one who knew a person's heart. We should treat everyone respectfully because Jesus valued every person.

I understood, but I battled against liking or disliking someone. I didn't like the Kilburn or Maynard children. They had made mean comments about me, and they were older and should know better. Charles Kilburn imitated my walk lumbering deep from side to side. Hanne said he'd imitated me well. The children who saw his imitation were either quiet or laughed. I begged Hanne to tell me who had been quiet or laughed. I wondered if my sisters had laughed. My face felt hot and my heart hurt.

Our teacher had heard a special flag presentation ceremony in Boston and wanted it part of our learning. Each day,
facing the American flag, we said, "I pledge allegiance to my
flag and to the Republic for which it stands, one nation, indi-
visible, with liberty and justice for all." We did practice drills
and review work for older students. We practiced math,
handwriting, vocabulary, geography, and read stories and
poems. Students took turns reading aloud. Not out of pride,
but because I heard others stumble over even some common
words, I thought I was among the best readers.

I breathed harder than normal when I limped back into
school from my noon trip to the outhouse. I had hurried, and
the air was colder. If I hurried when the weather was cold, I
felt a strain in my chest.

Miss MacIntosh asked for everyone's attention. Based on
our morning work, she would rearrange our seats. This
could be good or embarrassing. Only three people were
moved. Patience Crowenn, Hanne's friend, was moved
forward a row. Colleen Verling moved back to Ingelise's row,
and I was moved to Hanne's row.

Some students clapped. Others were shocked and
unhappy. Students started to make room for me beside
Hanne, but she grabbed her friends' hands and held them
close so I could not sit next to her. I kept a smile on my face
and sat at the end of the row.

We all had more work in the afternoon. Miss MacIntosh
walked among us, pointing out errors or encouraging us.
Suddenly the school day ended. I couldn't believe how fast
the day had flown. Miss MacIntosh gave us homework to
write goals for our year, map facts to review, and math problems. We each had a copy book in which to write our goals
and homework in our best handwriting. She'd read them the
next day while we studied.

Ingelise and Hanne sat far from me and whispered to the older students. When we arrived at the Y in the road by our house, Mr. Foster pulled the horses to a stop and lifted me down in one quick movement. I thanked him, and he tipped his hat to me. That was a thrill. He acted like I was a lady instead of a gimpy little girl.

Then the wagon moved, and I looked into our yard. Mama was in the yard with Ebba holding to her skirt. Ingelise and Hanne talked and talked as they ran to Mama. Mama smiled and let them chatter, but she lifted her eyes to look at me and give me a smile.

Every day, twenty- eight students sat in the classroom that was Dawson school. Absences were rare. Soon I knew my classmates' names and got along with most of them. My first year at Dawson was Ingelise's and another girl's last year. The two of them would go to the high school located in the town center and often talked about it on the way to Dawson and on the way home.

Holden's first high school had been a simple building, but in 1887, a Mr. Gale donated money to build a larger high school with a library. They built on Highland Street near the Congregational Church and the town hall.

I was surprised at the huge, impressive, brown-and-gray stone high school building. No other building in Holden was like it. The high school and library stood as a memorial to the Damon family, Mr. Gale's wife's family. The unique architectural design stood out boldly, but hardly anyone I talked to knew that Mr. Gale wanted the building made of local materials. Library patrons could use the door on the left, but we students had to enter through the door on the right.

The Damon Memorial building was dedicated on August 29, 1888

The first floor housed the library, and the second floor, the high school. I would attend the high school, and I planned to be the top student. While I couldn't play the physical games in the school yard, I could excel in the classroom. Every day at school, I strengthened this resolve.

I found out that students in high school classes all had to go up the large staircase to the second-floor rooms. I would not let the difficulty of stairs destroy my plan to achieve the highest possible grades and graduate as Valedictorian. That stood years ahead of me, but I knew I should build all the skills that would help me to reach my goal.

WITH SCHOOL AND FARMWORK, we rarely went into Worcester. Ingelise and Hanne had been in the Holden stores with Mama or Papa that the stores had lost interest for them. My older sisters had memories of the profusion of stores in Worcester and compared those to the small stores in Holden.

I had never been to Worcester stores but after a long stretch of school days, Mama and Papa liked to take us into town.

Holden had two stores. I had been in Harry Waite's general store a few times. Occasionally we had an extra penny or two, and we could spend it on candy or gum. Sometimes Papa let us use pennies for gum. Mama thought people should avoid gum, especially girls. "A gum chewing girl and a cud chewing cow, there is a difference I must allow. It's the intelligent look on the face of the cow," she would say.

6

TREATS, TALENTS, AND REJECTION

"Doves love treats. Some like to nibble on greens pinned to the bars of their cage....they also enjoy spray millet in their cages, cornbread, or whole wheat, cooked and cooled mashed sweet potato, cooked and cooled couscous, cottage cheese, shredded cheese, shredded carrots, and a hardboiled egg, cooled and mashed with the shell included (more added calcium!)" **Mary Ellen Robinson,** *International Dove Society*

I should have known not every school day would be like my first at Dawson. By October, I had a bad cold and missed two weeks of school. Just as I was planning to return, the first snow fell. It was less than a foot, but Mama and Papa decided I would attend school only two or three days a week when paths had been well cleared through the snow. I could do the work at home when I missed classes.

They said they didn't want me to tire myself or fall in the snow or on ice-covered areas. I knew Hanne and Ingelise told them about my difficult trek to the outhouse every day. My two older sisters sounded concerned for me as if they wanted to spare me undue strain. They sounded as if they cared about me when talking to Mama and Papa, but I knew they didn't really want me in school with them.

At least for comfort and fun I could play the piano while I was home. Ebba loved to sing in her light, high, and reedy voice. Her infant voice, to me, had been stronger. I did not think she would ever sing solos in public, but in a choir or singing duets, she would be fine. We had fun singing together every day that I had to stay home from school. I sang out loud and amused her at the piano for hours. I also showed Ebba how to do the household tasks I could do while sitting down.

Ingelise and Hanne didn't miss me at school. They looked sour-faced when they handed me Miss MacIntosh's notes, which had assignments with encouraging words. Sometimes she sent a book, sometimes her personal book to read and return. I read the books several times. There were myths from around the world, great plays, and famous books like *Uncle Tom's Cabin* and *Little Women*. I never had to write a book report on those books, but I wrote to tell her my thoughts on any loaned book.

The animals were warm in the hay-filled barn, and we were warm near the wood stove sending waves of heat, but it was not enough to warm the whole house. We spent our waking time in the kitchen. We girls slept in the one bed to try to stay warmer. Ingelise and Hanne got the edges with Ebba and me in the middle. Mama warmed bricks and a blanket by the oven. We carried them upstairs to the bed and then hurried into our nightgowns. We dove beneath the layers of covers to the brick-warmed areas.

Ingelise said rich people had warming pans with long handles. They were made of brass and filled with hot coals.

Holding the handle, a person rubbed the warming pans over the sheets, and the bed warmed.

I asked, "If they are so rich, why don't they have a way of keeping all the rooms in their mansion warm?"

She ignored my question as usual.

Whenever I hear *snug as a bug in a rug*, I think of sharing that bed with my sisters. We all rolled together and for a while, were thankful to be close. It was warm—piled like a bunch of puppies or a cluster of kittens.

When the winter continued cold weather and deep with snow, I felt trapped in the house. My sisters could sled, ice-skate, build snowmen and snow castles, snowshoe on Papa's homemade snow shoes, cross country ski with friends, and teach Ebba those sports. I couldn't even collect the eggs. Every morning Holden received a fresh coating of snow.

Often the older girls took Ebba outside. One time when they sledded down a hill, the ice beneath cracked at the bottom of the hill. The sled front went into freezing water. They screamed with surprise. In the house as they told their event, their story came out as a big adventure. They praised Ebba for laughing and not crying. I was proud of Ebba, but sad that she adventured outside without me.

That winter I tried to learn Danish. Mama and Papa received a Danish paper once a week. Mama translated stories for us. I asked her to show me the Danish words. We loved the continuing stories she translated. With few other entertainment options, reading stories was our excitement. Mama sometimes stretched the stories for days.

Learning Danish helped pass the time and was good for my brain, but learning a foreign language was a harder than I had expected. Studying Danish felt more difficult than learning the piano. By March I knew basic stories, songs, and poems.

In April the weather turned fair. I returned to school regularly. The exceptions were the days when the ground was too muddy. Some girls in my row welcomed me back, and Miss MacIntosh made me feel special. The other students didn't care a whit that I was there. That was fine. I was used to people choosing to ignore me.

When I started school, I decided I wouldn't get discouraged by people's negative reactions. If I let stares, whispers, a child's mimicking my walking bother me, I would become crippled inside. Why should I let other mean opinions affect me? I wouldn't.

Many people whispered opinions about my future. The general opinion held that a crippled young woman *should* stay at home, grateful for a caring family and shelter. The idea that a person, a girl especially, could have a career and live independently from her family was not accepted. For a crippled girl to have such hopes or dreams, it was seen as beyond ridiculous.

I wanted to learn, to attend high school, and maybe— to earn a special degree beyond high school. I yearned to be independent. I wanted qualification for work to earn my own living. I dreamed of a career because I couldn't imagine any young man wanting to marry me. Perhaps I could earn a living at a job that didn't require much physical exertion.

Most girls dreamed about the man they would marry, a house, how many children they would have. I thought about marriage, but not as much as being independent, involved in life, and admired for my personal strength, work, and abilities. My life wouldn't be much if I had to live as the crippled sister who never left home.

Ingelise talked about going to a Normal School which was like a community college, after high school. I didn't think she was smart enough for that but I did not say that to her or anyone. How could she get a degree beyond high school if she didn't enjoy reading?

Hanne earned decent marks but she didn't like education requirements. To me, Hanne seemed smarter than Ingelise. Unfortunately, Hanne admired Ingelise so much that she curbed her abilities and acted like a follower of Ingelise.

Ebba was interested in everything. She questioned me all the time. I loved her as my shadow. By four, she was my helper. She'd figured she could move things faster than I could, and she enjoyed fetching items for me. She anticipated what I needed physically like a full-time physical assistant.

On the cold, muddy days, Ebba let me lean on her to walk in the yard. Mama and Papa saw Ebba was a sweet- spirited younger sister. I agreed. I was thankful she enjoyed being with me and helping me. Plus, she never made me feel like a burden.

In May, Miss MacIntosh planned a program for the last school day. The parents were invited. The parents wanted their children to be exemplary citizens who knew how to read, speak, write, math, and had good values. The program would display their talents.

Miss MacIntosh gave each of us a part. Some parts were short, given to students who were glad not to say much. Everyone made decorations. The shy twins said the flag pledge together. Ingelise, the eldest student and most lady-like, gave the welcome. Four boys were ushers. The youngest children gave a presentation on the ABCs of famous Americans. Hanne and four friends gave a skit about honesty. A trio of girls sang. Then a quartet of girls sang a song. Nelson McGann recited the Gettysburg address.

I loved Miss MacIntosh's stories of real people like Emma Lazarus. Emma Lazarus captured my heart. She was born to Spanish Jews, who had immigrated to New York City. She felt the prejudice against Jews, but decided to live proud of her heritage. She wrote poems and dramas, all showing her ancestral pride. I knew how it felt to be judged of something I couldn't control. I didn't believe I could ever feel proud of being crippled, yet I hoped to feel proud in spite of it.

Three girls recited the words on the Statue of Liberty's base. Emma Lazarus had written the words, entitled 'The New Colossus.' The girls practiced the words in unison. Since many of us were children of immigrants, the words of 'The New Colossus' had special meaning. I wondered how long it took Emma Lazarus to compose such fine words of hope.

Not like the brazen giant of Greek fame with conquering limbs astride from land to land; Here at our sea-washed, sunset gates shall stand

A mighty woman with a torch, whose flame Is the imprisoned lightning, and her name Mother of Exiles. From her beacon-hand Glows world-wide welcome; her mild eyes command the air-bridged harbor that twin cities frame, "Keep, ancient lands, your storied pomp!" cries she with silent lips. "Give me your tired, your poor, Your huddled masses yearning to breathe free, the wretched refuse of your teeming shore, Send these, the homeless, tempest-tossed to me, I lift my lamp beside the golden door!"

Would I ever see these words engraved on a plaque on the Statue of Liberty's base? I told myself that when I grew up, I'd earn money to visit other cities. I loved public speaking if I could stand and talk. I did not want to walk to the front of a room in front of people's stares.

The part I wanted to say was George Washington's Prayer for the Nation. Chills coursed through my body the first time I read its words. Miss MacIntosh gave that prayer to Stephen Springdale. Stephen spoke slowly and without emotion. Miss MacIntosh worked with him on improving his dramatic ability. I memorized the words too because I loved them.

> Almighty God, we make our earnest prayer that Thou wilt keep the United States in thy holy protection that Thou wilt incline the hearts of the citizens to cultivate a spirit of subordination and obedience to government and entertain a brotherly affection and love for one another and for their fellow citizens of the United States at large. And finally, that Thou wilt most graciously be pleased to dispose us all to do justice, to love mercy, and to demean ourselves with that charity, humility, and pacific temper of mind which were the characteristics of the Divine Author of our blessed religion, and without a humble imitation of whose example in these things, we can never hope to be a happy nation.
>
> Grant our supplication, we beseech Thee, through Jesus Christ our Lord. Amen."

Stephen teetered between a soft or loud monotone. I told Miss MacIntosh if Stephen got sick, I was ready to give the prayer. She just smiled and said thank you.

My part was to recite the opening paragraphs of the Declaration of Independence and the preamble to the US Constitution. I was young to have this part, but Miss MacIntosh thought I could memorize and present it with expression. With her confidence in me, I could not imagine failing. I practiced in front of little Ebba and on my own.

By the night of the program, Ebba with all seriousness, thinking she was reciting correctly could say, "When a course of humans is necessary people dissolve." Her mimicry had me smiling.

The actual words I recited were:

> When in the Course of human events, it becomes necessary for one people to dissolve the political bands which have connected them with another, and to assume among the powers of the earth, the separate and equal station to which the Laws of Nature and of Nature's God entitle them, a decent respect to the opinions of mankind requires that they should declare the causes which impel them to the separation.
>
> We hold these truths to be self-evident, that all men are created equal, that they are endowed by their Creator with certain unalienable Rights that among these are Life, Liberty and the pursuit of Happiness."

How I enjoyed proclaiming this!

Then I went on to say, "We the People of the United States, in order to form a more perfect Union, establish Justice, insure domestic Tranquility, provide for the common defense, promote the general Welfare, and secure the Blessings of Liberty to ourselves and our Posterity, do ordain and establish this Constitution for the United States of America."

Miss MacIntosh trusted me to make the thoughts clear by my expression and by pausing in the correct places. I never worried about forgetting lines. Once I had them memorized, they stuck in my head like when I memorized a piano piece after I playing it a half a dozen times.

This year we had studied American history, and the parents would know that from our program. We wanted to give a good performance for Miss MacIntosh. I hoped to have her for my teacher for all the years I attended Dawson.

Single women teachers who married had to relinquish their teaching career. I didn't understand this. We wondered why our teacher didn't have a beau. She was lively, smart, kind, and pretty. Yet we didn't want her to marry; we'd lose her. The female teachers who got married moved to the job of wife, homemaker, and probably soon the job of mother.

I thought Miss MacIntosh was too good as a teacher to stay at home for a husband. My mother seemed happy with Papa and children, but I doubted Mama had wanted another career besides a family. She hadn't trained for any career, so she had to clean houses, take in ironing, and sew clothing for other people to earn money.

I became so excited about the school program that I became feverish. Mama said my face looked flushed at dinner.

"Annelise, are you feeling overheated?"

"I'm fine, Mama." I didn't want to miss the program.

Papa interrupted, "You will do just fine, Annelise. You have a mind and heart for details and a personality for drama. Ebba loves your stories. We all enjoy your music almost as much as Mama's piano playing. Mama and I will be proud of you, Hanne, and Ingelise tonight."

And they were.

We would have our summer vacation after this program. I started my vacation sick. When we got home, I did feel feverish. I was sick for three days. Mama guessed it came from extreme excitement, but I couldn't believe that. At least I would have the summer break to recover and looked forward to the school year ahead with our wonderful Miss MacIntosh.

After just two weeks into our new school year, Ingelise came running in the house. She had been visiting two other girls who attended high school with her. They lived closer to the center of town.

"Guess what? Miss MacIntosh is going to get married next June!"

MISS MACINTOSH BECAME ENGAGED to Stanley Washburn, a wealthy, well-educated young businessman. She was the first career woman I had known. Her family wasn't rich. I thought she really enjoyed teaching, but she gave it up to marry a man. *Why can't a woman be happy without a husband?*

Why did the town leaders insist a married woman could not continue teaching? Married people could love one another have careers. Miss MacIntosh could be a teacher and a wife.

Looking at Mama and Papa, I couldn't imagine one without the other. Married people could show what the Bible meant about being one. Mama and Papa reminded me of Philemon and Baucis, Greek peasants who shared what they had with strangers. Though my parents didn't want me to tell many myths or fairytales to Ebba, Mama and Papa reminded me of the intertwined devotion and selflessness of Baucis and Philemon when I read how hard they worked together and helped people in need of food, clothes, and shelter. They did this especially through the Baptist Church services to the community, and all the efforts were crucial especially in the winter.

We had a stretch of zero- degree days without snow. I could attend school because of no drifts, slush, and only a little ice. I bundled in layers to be warmer and went happily to school each cold, clear day.

I wanted to give Miss MacIntosh a special Christmas gift.

Ingelise and Hanne said everyone gave teachers a Christmas card. In our school the cards were handmade with great care. Mama gave us scraps of ribbon and yarn to decorate our cards. I put a sprig of holly with berries on mine.

Our Christmas celebrations were simple. Papa cut a Christmas tree from the woods. We children could accompany him. Even I could go along, but always I stayed home. Mama had a magical touch and extra energy around Christmas for baking.

The house was fragrant with scents that made my mouth water. I sampled everything Mama baked in various stages. For a hot drink, only Postum was available. Mama and Papa didn't drink coffee and tea. They thought Postum contained healthier ingredients. Mama also made a special spiced, Danish drink and ginger snap cookies for Christmas time.

The heart was a traditional Danish symbol. Mama knew crafts from her youth in Denmark. That Christmas, the last I would have with Miss MacIntosh, I sat at the kitchen table cutting red-and-white hearts to decorate the downstairs rooms, but also to make an elaborate card for my teacher.

I told Mama I longed to take some of her Christmas goodies to Miss MacIntosh. Mama helped me fix a beautiful plate of her Danish Pebber Nodder, cookies like bites of Christmas delight. They were a shortbread recipe with cinnamon and cardamom flavor. Ginger snaps were added to the plate and a shower of my tiny, paper, red-and-white hearts dropped over the cookies. The hearts reminded me of confetti.

"These are many cookies for one school teacher," Mama said, smiling as she wrapped my decorated brown paper over the plate. "I think your teacher will enjoy this treat for days. It's a lovely gift."

"Delicious, too, thanks, Mama. I really wanted to give

Miss MacIntosh more than a card. She works hard with us and this is her last year as our teacher."

"Annelise, when you finish making the string of hearts for Miss MacIntosh, will you let Ingelise and Hanne sign their names on the hearts? It can be a gift from all three of you with the plate of cookies, like a gift from our whole family." The cookies used fine baking flour, sugar, and spices.

"Of course, Mama." I should have offered without Mama's request. I carefully carried the plate to the oak chest near the door. We couldn't afford three such gifts. Mama wouldn't want only one daughter to give our teacher a fine present. It didn't matter if Ingelise and Hanne wanted to give a gift besides their card. Mama wanted the gift from all three of us.

CHRISTMAS WAS on a Saturday in 1915. The world did not feel Christmas joy because of a terrible war in Europe. In May a German submarine sank an ocean liner, the *Lusitania*. Why would they sink a ship that was not a war ship?

**Drawing of the Lusitania from National Defense
Canadian Navy**

Mama and Papa followed news in Europe through the

Danish and Worcester newspapers. The Danish people remained neutral during the war. I didn't understand the war, but I figured that Germany wanted to take over other countries. It had captured Belgium, Hungary, Austria, Serbia, and Bulgaria. The Germans had attacked Russia and France. Britain fought in the war. Miss MacIntosh explained that Britain, Russia, and France were allied to help one another against their enemy, Germany, even in North Africa.

Ingelise didn't care about the war. Hanne never let me see if she cared. She talked mostly with Ingelise and Ebba. Did my older sisters ignore what happened in the world?

Papa said Britain held Germans from taking over everywhere. Canadians and some Americans had joined Britain in fighting the Germans. Many Americans wanted to join the fighting after the Lusitania was sunk. President Woodrow Wilson had been against the war.

Awful battles had taken place, especially one sad slaughter at Gallipoli, a place in the Mediterranean. I couldn't find the place on our school maps. I was frustrated that most grown- ups didn't want to talk about the war in front of children.

In our house on Christmas 1915, no hint of war was present. Mama and Papa kept a great fire in the stove. Glowing warmth filled the kitchen and spilled into the front room. Some of that heat pushed up the stairs toward our room. When the deep cold arrived, we leaped out of bed— even I tumbled out— and ran to wash in the warmth of the kitchen at black stone sink. I scooted downstairs on my bottom as fast as Ebba could run.

Even on Christmas we washed and dressed before we went to look under the Christmas tree in the dining room. We saw two packages for each person. Oranges—large and sweet, another treat in the cold week of Christmas, sat on tree branches, one for each of us. The presents under the tree were wrapped in new scarves Mama had knit. Ingelise received a dark gold one. Hanne got a bright blue one. Mine was red, my favorite color. Ebba's was a mixture of the other colors. It didn't matter that our gifts were practical items like stockings. They were fine and beautiful.

I squeezed the scarf to see if the inside gift was soft or hard. Mine was very firm. I hugged it to me and smiled at Mama and Papa. The only flat hard item I had picked from the Sears Catalog was a bound journal with a beautiful cover. My sisters and I had spent hours looking through the Sears Roebuck catalog and gave a few ideas to Mama and Papa.

The journal unwrapped reminded me of rich volumes I had seen in libraries. Miss MacIntosh said I had beautiful handwriting. I would use my best writing for thoughts and dreams, observations and questions, songs, and poems, in my beautiful present.

7

CHOICES WHISPERS, STAIRS, AND STARES

"In the book of Genesis, it is the dove which brought Noah news of dry land. In the book of Leviticus, the dove has the questionable honor of being considered clean enough to be used as a sacrifice." **Wendell M. Levi, *Encyclopedia of Pigeon Breeds***

The year I turned 15—1920—I was a third-year student at the high school located above the Gale Free Library. Some students left school after eighth grade to work on family farms or in family businesses. Five of us chose to continue in high school.

In 1920 the 19th amendment passed, giving women the right to vote. The country also voted for prohibition, restricting the sale of alcoholic drinks. Mama and Papa hoped that was a sign people would turn from sinful living. I thought people found ways around the prohibition laws just like we all did around rules we did not like.

More cars on the roads. Some cost $300. Papa didn't want a car. He preferred a horse and wagon. He purchased a cart for us girls and Mama to drive. Papa taught us how to hitch Jenny, our energetic young horse, to the cart. I loved the independence to drive in that cart, though I only took it when I had to be somewhere and no one could accompany me.

Women's opportunities were changing in our nation but not in our household or town. Most people on Bailey Road cooked on wood stoves and in brick ovens, even though new appliances were available. I read about the stoves, refrigerators, and washing machines in catalogues and newspapers. No one on our road even had electricity, but we heard electricity would come soon.

Holden built a hospital in 1918, which made us think we were progressing, but no one could afford to be sick. Spanish influenza and scarlet fever circulated our area that year. Scarlet fever was more feared, but to the great relief of everyone, not many folks contracted it.

When I wanted to discuss how Woodrow Wilson had taken our country through the World War I years, no one at school cared. Even the teachers wouldn't discuss anything outside our curriculum. If I had been a boy, my history teacher might have talked with me. Only Papa discussed his views on people and historical events with me.

Mama participated with women from the town churches in planning a celebration of Thanksgiving for the end of World War I, held shortly after Armistice Day, November 11, 1918. The town erected a memorial to honor those from Holden who had served in WWI. One hundred twenty-seven people, including one woman, had served, and five local men had died. The monument—with the veterans' names inscribed—was located between the Gale building and the First Congregational Church.

New people moved to Holden. Many were rich and the

houses built showed a size and quality equal to the best houses in Worcester. Some people who moved to Holden from Worcester tried to purchase small tracks of land for farms, but they did not have riches. Land developers bought land and built housing communities that had streets like labyrinths.

Papa had earned over $750 the previous year. Even with that much money, he could barely pay the mortgage and take care of our family needs, animals, and equipment because he had also purchased adjoining acres. He said land was healthy for a family to work and was a good investment. He had a future goal for the farm and us.

I overheard Mama and Papa talk about giving land to each daughter and her husband. They seemed to expect their daughters and husbands to settle and build houses on their gifted property. I don't remember them mentioning my name in connection to *married daughters*. The clutch of a pain around my heart I dismissed because I knew they were real-istic parents.

High school excited me. The students came from other towns, but difficulties came when the girls talked and cared about looks and clothes. My shabby hand-me- downs kept me from acceptance. The new affluent students were imme-diately popular and the social leaders. Even without being poor, my limp and twisted foot relegated me almost invisible.

Ebba asked me about my days in high school. Only with her did I share a little of my loneliness and self-conscious-ness. I wanted her to admire me. I was worried she might hear about my struggle every day going up the school stairs. Someone would talk about it. The steps were a daily torture. I knew about elevators but it could be years before the Gale building had one if it ever did. Still, I resolved never to show my misery.

High school was a giant step. Some people's expectations settled on finishing eighth grade. Mama and Papa were proud of my academic accomplishments. I wanted to graduate a year early, so I studied with an intensity my classmates did not understand.

After high school, I didn't know what I would do, but I wanted good choices. Though my grades were excellent, my school accomplishments were no big news. In the past years, we had faced unusual surprises, mostly with Ingelise.

During my first high school year, Ingelise had completed a course study in Framingham at a Normal School, one of the first in the state. It later became the largest state teachers' college. Framingham offered a variety of programs, some academic and some practical. Ingelise took a dietician's course. The family realized she would have flunked if I hadn't helped her on major projects.

Mama confessed that to me, but not to Ingelise that Ingelise was grateful for my help. It was just difficult for her to say thank you, to acknowledge her younger crippled sister had helped with essential work.

Ingelise worked as a certified dietician with a hospital. She shared an apartment with three other young women, who worked at the hospital. Being a career woman and sharing an apartment with girlfriends sounded wonderful to me, a real reward for completing the dietician program. Then Ingelise took a job far away. She didn't have friends to share apartment costs, but she considered that and managed on her earnings.

Hanne started nursing courses in Worcester during my second year of high school. I helped her with school work.

Even Ebba helped. Ebba was as smart as I had guessed her to be, but she was shy and quiet. No one knew Ebba's intelligence until they talked or listened to her. She had a great sense of humor and heart kinder than anyone I knew. Being at home, we tutored Hanne in practice with facts and studies for tests. Hanne rewarded us all when she was qualified as an RN.

Ingelise wrote to Hanne a couple of times a week, but Hanne did not share much news even when asked. I asked most often because I could see the sadness in Mama and Papa.

"Hanne, are you going to share Ingelise's news at supper?"

"Not much to say."

"Why doesn't Ingelise write to anyone else, especially not to Mama and Papa?"

"She's busy. She hasn't so much extra time to write letters."

"What does she do after work every day?"

Hanne just smiled at me and moved away to work on something for herself or Mama. No surprise showed in Hanne when in the spring of my second high school year, Ingelise came home with a handsome Italian beau. She had met him soon after moving to Harrisburg. Now I knew what Ingelise had been doing with all her time after work.

Anthony, Ingelise's beau, had a profile like Michelangelo Buonarroti's, *David*. Although Ingelise was attractive with the dark hair, eyes, and pale skin Mama had, I felt surprised she had captured the attention of a man as good looking as Anthony. He was polite, more polite than Papa. The manners Anthony displayed were gentlemanly and like characters I had read about in novels set in Europe.

Soon we realized that Papa acted remote toward Anthony. Did Papa felt concerned because Anthony was the first beau to meet our family, to come to ask to marry Papa's eldest daughter? Could Papa be prejudiced against a son of Italian immigrants?

No. I knew. Papa didn't have prejudices against ethnic groups. But in the two days Anthony visited us, Papa excused himself to do work out in the barn. Papa knew Ingelise and Anthony were serious about one another.

The first day we all got acquainted with simple conversation. Anthony had finished his plumber's apprenticeship. He seemed like a hard worker. His skill could support a wife and a family. Anthony slept on the porch cot after the first day he and Ingelise visited. The second day he met with Mama and Papa while Ebba and I were at school. Anthony asked permission to marry Ingelise.

We learned about this when we arrived home from school that Ingelise and Anthony had left. Papa had said no to Anthony's request, and Mama agreed with Papa. Hanne, Ebba, and I had expected we might have a celebratory supper, but now it was a sad household.

Why? Mama and Papa had always warned us about prejudices in Worcester County. Papa especially didn't respect a big Worcester company, the Norton Company, because of a song Norton employees sang against hiring Hungarians, Italians, and Poles. Both Papa and Mama valued hospitality and tried to make people feel welcome. How did this change?

Normally the marriage of a daughter, almost twenty, made the parents happy. Hanne was silent and angry. Ebba was confused. I could not be silent. I had to ask. Mama and Papa were in the kitchen when I asked my question.

"Mama, Papa, will you tell me why you do not want Ingelise to marry Anthony?"

Mama put her sewing down, and Papa put his Bible aside.

"Anthony is Catholic," Papa said.

"Ingelise has to convert, to become Catholic, to take their

training and convert to have a marriage with Anthony that will be legal to the Catholic church and to his family." Mama explained in the saddest voice I had ever heard from her.

Pain appeared in my parents' eyes and faces. I wondered if they had had as much pain in their expressions when their once normal daughter was crippled. Suddenly I doubted my crippled condition was as awful to them as Ingelise converting to another religion.

Catholicism had different beliefs and customs from Nazarene and Baptist, the two churches Ingelise had been raised in, Nazarene until we moved to Holden, and then Baptist because of the Holden First Baptist Church. To Mama and Papa, conversion to Catholicism was taking a huge step backwards. Protestants paid more attention to the Bible and Jesus and believed Christians lived in a direct relationship with God. Catholics paid more attention to the words of the Pope, to Mary, and counted on priests, saints, and dead relatives to intercede with God for them. To Catholics, it was a rare, hard road for one to become a saint. To Protestants, New Testament scriptures said all who confessed Jesus as their Savior and Lord were saints.

My confusion grew. I had met some Catholic people who believed Jesus was their Lord and Savior, but I knew they did pray to Mary and saints, not just to Jesus. To Catholics, the Church had the final say on any matter. Average people could not read and understand the Bible on their own, according to Catholics. To Protestants, the Bible was the authority one used. Everyone was to read the Bible. Jesus promised to send the Holy Spirit to all His followers. The Spirit brought each believer understanding of the Word of God.

Catholics believed babies must be baptized to enter heaven. To Protestants, baptism was a symbol to follow

Christ. A person made this public through baptism because for Protestants baptism stood as the symbol of commitment to follow Jesus. It did not affect one's entering heaven. God would always accept babies and anyone else who didn't know the difference between good and evil.

Catholic friends had told me about purgatory. This idea made it seem like an in-between place that did not appear in the Bible worked like a waiting room for people who still had to have people pray for them. The prayers would eventually cause them to leave purgatory and go into heaven. Could Ingelise believe this or would she just say she did to make some priest happy and to have an acceptable wedding for the Catholic church and Anthony's family? I thought she would probably say anything to marry Anthony.

Mama and Papa were crushed that Ingelise switched religions so easily. I wasn't worried about Ingelise's soul. I wondered if her faith in words and deeds had been honest. Maybe Ingelise had no set faith. Maybe she had even just gone through the motions to please Mama and Papa. Maybe Catholicism was really her faith, her first choice of belief. We believed in the same God, the Bible, Jesus, and the disciples. Would this change cut Ingelise off from our family? Should it?

Anthony was savvy. He understood our folks were unhappy he was Catholic. I thought he knew they blamed him for Ingelise's conversion. friends, and church.

After they left us, Hanne shared the news that Ingelise planned to live with Anthony's older, married sister until the wedding, and he continued to live with his parents. A month later, they married in a Catholic church in Harrisburg, Pennsylvania. I expected Ingelise liked living in a city, especially a state capitol. We had studied state capitols. President Teddy

Roosevelt had spoken at the capitol's dedication in Harrisburg in 1906.

President Teddy Roosevelt was one of my favorite leaders. When I asked Ebba what she thought about him, she said, "I think you like him because he was sick so much as a child. He had to miss lots of school like you. He worked hard, had many achievements, and became an outgoing person totally overcoming his childhood health problems. That's what you plan to do, isn't it, Annelise?"

Ebba appeared meek and mild, but she had a disturbing ability to see into me and even into other people. I knew better than to judge people by appearances, but looks meant a lot to me. Ebba looked past the surface appearances and she had a happiness even though people could be so disquieting.

I was thankful for things in my life. But happy? I often squashed my emotions. Most times, it was too painful to reflect on happiness. I wanted to be a good daughter and make my parents proud especially since I had given them heartache and extra expenses. I wanted to be smart to find a career to support myself, to help take care of them, and not be the crippled daughter at home with aging parents.

Because of Ingelise's conversion and marriage, my parents' relationship seemed shadowed by a strain of grief. I wondered if Mama fully agreed with Papa. None of us attended the wedding. That was another big surprise. No matter their disappointment, I thought one of them would take the train to the wedding.

The wedding took place in a Catholic church and a priest did the ceremony. My parents had never been in a Catholic church, and said they had no desire to visit one. They carried a grief like Ingelise had died. It seemed wrong.

Ingelise sent Ebba and me money at Christmas and on our birthdays until we finished schooling. We wrote her thank you notes. Mine always sounded stiff, but Ebba's were sweeter and more open with news and affection. She had Mama's grace and continued to be kindness personified. Ebba brought Ingelise's name in conversation more than anyone else.

Since Anthony Albert Trombino had a large family, I supposed they had welcomed and loved Ingelise. I hoped that was true. All Italians I had met seemed more expressive and affectionate than our family.

Most of the time Ingelise was out of my consciousness. She had chosen another family, another religion, another state. She had chosen to leave us, and if that caused pain, then I wouldn't think about her. The rest of Ingelise's life, she and Mama exchanged only a couple of letters a year.

Papa never talked about Ingelise. When we did, he only listened. I wondered what Mama's and Papa's true feelings were about their decision and actions toward Anthony.

Then in 1917, we learned that Mama was pregnant. She showed joy in having another child. I could see and hear her the moment she told Ebba and me about the baby at breakfast one school day. Papa had left for his job in Worcester. She sat at the table with an unusual expression on her face. "Girls, I have some special news for you." She was nervous but excited. She looked younger and happier.

Unable to subdue her delight, Mama said, "You are *both* going to be older sisters before the year is over." Ebba and I looked at each other, then at Mama who had a beaming smile and no blush at all.

Ebba would lose her place as the baby of the family. But absolute joy covered Ebba's countenance when she heard a baby would be born. Ebba had no jealous possessiveness of her position as baby of the family. I felt shocked but tried not to show that emotion.

Mama stopped cleaning houses, but still sewed for folks. Papa had added many acres over the years, eighty-five in total. He sold eggs, hay, vegetables, currants, raspberries, and blueberries since our property produced an abundance. He added peach trees. Papa also worked as a machinist in Worcester and did repair or small carpentry jobs independently.

I wondered how this unexpected baby would change our lives. I wrote to Ingelise. I wanted her to know she would be a big sister again and only months after she had her first baby! Ingelise had a girl named Elenora in September of 1919. The name was for a special person in Anthony's family. Italians liked to name children after beloved relatives. I thought Ingelise's letters seemed more caring after she became a mother, but our parents' judgement, the distance, and past experiences worked against me having a better relationship with her.

The Danish had a similar custom to Italians of naming a child after a deceased family member. Other popular options included naming the child after a Norse god or goddess or a great hero and giving a child many names. In many early 1900 Danish families, children were given four and five names.

Mama and Papa were exceptional in that they named their children after gifts from God. Ingelise meant *God's grace*. Her middle name, Esther, was after Mama's relative. Hanne meant *God's gift*. Her middle name was Karen and meant *pure*. My name Annelise meant *graceful light* and suited me when I was born, but not now. I was not graceful and had dark eyes and hair. I felt wounded that I didn't live up to my name's meaning. My middle name was Marti, which meant *lady*. Ebba's name meant *strength*, and she was strong in her quiet way. Inger, her middle name, meant *daughter of a hero*. I liked that. Ebba never commented on her name. She lived her name's meaning.

Names seemed to me like a path into knowing a person's background. Lots of people knew that Joren, our surname, came from the cold northlands, but they didn't know if it was Danish, Finnish, Swedish, or Norwegian. I liked that Joren was easy to spell.

Mama wanted to see her first grandchild and help Ingelise. She told that to me and Ebba one gray afternoon when I helped Ebba make supper. It must have hurt Mama to know she wasn't needed. Anthony's parents and grandparents lived in their neighborhood. Anthony also had many sisters who helped. If Ingelise had invited her, Mama would have traveled to Pennsylvania, but Ingelise never did.

Ebba and I had noticed Mama had been quieter since Ingelise had left us. Even with some letters, I thought Mama felt regret. If I ever had a child, would anything make me reject that child? Mama and Papa must have thought often of Ingelise, their firstborn. I knew they prayed for her, Anthony, and the granddaughter they had never seen.

Ingelise invited Hanne to visit, and Hanne planned to go in spring after she completed her nursing program. By then Hanne would have seen her new sister or brother and could tell Ingelise about the baby. When she returned, she could tell us about our first niece, Elenora.

Families were important even when relationships brought pain. How did Ingelise choose Anthony over Mama and Papa and her sisters? I was confused by love—people sought it, said love fulfilled them—yet it caused hurt and disappointment.

I wasn't as brave as Mama in loving others. She devoted

her life to being a wonderful wife and mother. She believed we honored God when we handled our responsibilities well and cared for other people generously. Many times, we must have caused her fear and distress and she still loved us.

But was it a good time for Mama to be pregnant? She seemed too old, but who wants to say that to a pregnant woman? Why were she and Papa physically intimate at their age? Papa was forty-six, and Mama, forty-four. That's not a comment a fifteen-year-old says to her parent. I wondered how Mama had told Papa about the pregnancy. Maybe a husband could tell if his wife was pregnant by how his wife looked and moved.

When Mama told us, Ebba had said instantly, "Oh Mama! That's wonderful. I'll love having a baby in the house. I've always wanted to be a big sister!"

Tears filled Mama's eyes. Ebba rushed to hug Mama.

No one expected me to rush to do anything.

I stared at them and composed a happy face. If women had a choice about having babies, I figured Mama had made a wrong one. People should have babies while they were young, not as old as Mama and Papa. Grown-ups—Would I ever understand them?

What would I do as an adult. Marry? Have children? What man would have me? Would I fall for the first man who courted me? I hadn't seen a crippled married person. Pudge, I was not only crippled, but chubby.

"Oh, I'm glad you girls are happy about this," Mama said. "Look at the time. You girls finish breakfast and then get into your coats. You don't want to miss your rides."

Ebba was still taking Mr. Foster's wagon to the elementary school, but I took the high school *barge*, a horse-drawn, flat-bed wagon. The students from the town's poor side rode this transportation. I was embarrassed to struggle to climb into it. The driver dropped a wood block of two steps to help me board.

The students on the school barge stared or looked away when I got on. Some talked in animation as if my slowness affected their speech. I wished if one boy leaped off as a gentleman and gave me a hand up, he would be my knight. No boy even thought of that.

During my first year at high school, a younger man drove the barge and placed the wood steps down for me. Then he got off the wagon and helped me aboard. I tried not to fall in love, so I settled on a crush. I raved to Ebba about him, his kindness and strength. His looks didn't matter like his attitude and actions. Then he moved to Hopkinton, and our present barge driver arrived.

Some days the driver didn't put the wood steps down for me. Other students hopped on quickly. I hated asking him, but I had to ask. The wagon bed was beyond my reach.

Nothing physically improved for me at the Gale building. The high school classes were held on the second floor. Everyone, except me, leapt off the wagon and hurried inside.

There were two flights of stairs, one to a landing, and another to the second floor. I leaned against the banister and hauled myself up using both hands to pull up with the help of the railing. Mama had made me a satchel to free my hands.

By the time I reached the second floor, the students had hung their coats, hats, and scarves and were in their seats, starting the morning work from the blackboard. I tried to block the thought of them while I took off my wraps. Why couldn't one friendly person, a girl my age, wait with me as I struggled up the steps? I didn't expect any boy ever would help me.

Often, I caught someone looking at me to see how I

coped. Someday I'd move better. I didn't know how, but I would search for a way to be freer and smoother in walking.

Most days by the time I walked to my seat, the teacher had taken roll and walked between the students' rows, looking at their work. She never spoke about my pace, never made a comment that might push me to hurry. None of the teachers pressured or embarrassed me.

Only my feelings did that. Every day embarrassment reinforced my resolve to be the top student. I wanted it known that a cripple was the best student, that the girl they ignored had passed them in every subject. Was that mean and unchristian? I think so, but I felt that I **had to** achieve honors.

My desk was closest to the stairs and to the coat room. That was assigned to me out of a teacher's kindness. Perhaps the teachers understood I lived in fear of falling each day. Yet they didn't know my right hip and side were sore from trying to move quicker while I was in school. Sometimes my back ached terribly with all the muscles working to compensate for the small right leg and twisted foot.

I was the only crippled person most of the students knew. They might meet others. When they did, they would think of me. I wanted them to remember I was brave, willing to step forward with a twisted foot and crippled leg. I wanted everyone to know people with physical disabilities possessed other strong abilities. I could do many things well. I would be true to myself, depend on God, and try to ignore the stares and occasional mean whispers.

8

DESPERATE FOR CHANGE

"Leg bands, or rings, as they are called in Great Britain, are the markers on the legs of the doves by which the breeder can identify each bird….seamless bands are metal rings usually made of aluminum. They are made in varying sizes to fit any breed of pigeon/dove." **Wendell M. Levi,** *Encyclopedia of Pigeon Breeds*

The trip in and out the high school, plus my daily steps, made me more tired than I had expected. At one day's end, I found myself alone upstairs, far behind the others. As I leaned against at the banister, an idea flashed through my mind. Unladylike as it sounded and with my satchel across my back, I slipped my body onto the banister and whoa! I was downstairs in seconds. If I hadn't been afraid of falling, the ride would have been fun. That saved me precious minutes and awkward clumping downstairs.

As spring of my junior year blossomed, I decided I would exercise to strengthen my leg. I hoped the exercises would also straighten my foot and lessen my limp. I craved walking better at my graduation ceremony. I had decided near the beginning of high school to graduate a year early. After two and a half years, I was consistently the top academic student. I knew I could do the required work to graduate a year early.

Something else drove me to finish within three years. Only a few weeks into high school, I broke into a cold sweat at the thought Ebba would start high school when I was still there. She'd see how the others treated me. She would want to help me, ease my embarrassment or physical strain. I didn't want that responsibility on her. I didn't want her tied to me, pitied, and isolated. I needed to be out so she could find her identity and make friends. She was shy, but others would see her goodness.

For me, Ebba was my sister and my friend; that was enough. When I attended a college or business school, I would meet people who perceived me from a positive viewpoint. I needed them before I turned bitter.

At home in the attic, I sorted through equipment and shoes Mama and Papa had bought me over the years. I hadn't used any of the equipment daily in at least a year. An uncomfortable foot brace had chaffed my skin but had made a slight improvement. Perhaps the device might straighten my foot if I wore it longer.

MAMA'S last baby was a boy. They named him Axel. I know Mama was grateful to God the baby was a son. She loved to give Papa enjoyable surprises. Axel was her greatest surprise for Papa.

Papa had been full of joy at the news of a son. We thought he might rise and float out of the house. We girls knew he loved us. Now though, late in life, he would have his son at home in his older years. Farmers counted on a son to help them with the huge amount of work.

Axel was healthy and sturdy with alert hazel eyes, thick dark hair, a happy personality, and a strong spirit. As a baby, he hardly cried. Ebba and I thought he might be our family's smartest child. He was a bright point in all our lives. In English, an axel was a part of a vehicle, but in Danish, Axel meant *vigilant,* a strong name for a boy.

In the dim, cold, stuffy attic, my attitude brightened as I thought on Axel. Cheerfully, I tried on the various leg support pieces. Finally, I settled on the brace with metal rings and a steel support rod. I clomped around the attic, then to our bedroom.

Ebba watched as I arrived. "I wondered what you were doing."

"Maybe I gave up on this brace too soon," I told her, looking down at the device.

"You wore it for almost two years," she reminded me.

"That might not have been long enough."

"You might be right," she agreed. "With all that metal, is it heavy?"

"Not as heavy as it sounds." We both laughed.

We went downstairs and into the kitchen. Ebba walked lightly. I clomped behind her.

Axel was in his highchair that Papa had constructed for his first Christmas present. Axel was born a week before Thanksgiving, so now at six months, he sat in it like a little king. We were his attendants and didn't mind.

I stood next to him as he played with a hard biscuit on the tray.

"Annelise, you're trying that brace again?" Mama asked.

"Yes, Mama. It fits better now. I want to try it a few months. I could move better if this makes my foot straighter. I want to walk more gracefully."

She didn't say anything to me, but she sighed in a way that said everything.

The brace suddenly felt heavier. I *would* wear it. I *would* exercise, walk, practice, and get stronger. I *would* make progress. They'd see.

In a week Hanne left for Harrisburg to stay with Ingelise, Anthony, and Elenora. She intended to look for a job there; I had heard her tell a friend. I knew she hadn't told Mama or Papa. If they knew her plans, they would fear she'd meet and marry a Catholic.

Having Axel would help us continue our daily lives. He had a natural curiosity about everything and a kind heart. Did I ever have that sweetness I wondered.

MY DETERMINATION WAS as strong as fire. I did chapters and projects in all subjects at a record pace. My teachers reported to my parents they had never seen a student as motivated as I was for every course and assignment.

By April I knew my goal of early graduation was within reach. I heard my teachers talking when the students were outside. They sat and chatted in a corner area. I sat quietly to the side, keeping my head down and working. Somehow, they overlooked my presence. With my disability, I was an invisible person. The teachers talked softly, but I could hear.

"Annelise Joren is the top student again after this quarter's exams," began one teacher.

"She does amazing work and has beautiful handwriting," commented another.

"It looks as if she will complete all the required studies by June."

"She told me she wanted to graduate early," Miss Larson, my favorite teacher, said.

"If she is valedictorian, she will give a fine speech."

All the teachers fell silent but exchanged uncomfortable glances.

"Annelise is the top student. Why shouldn't she be valedictorian?" Miss Larson asked. She was one of the toughest but most fair in evaluating students.

Silence pervaded the room. I knew their thoughts. They were picturing the valedictorian clomping with a rocking gait to the podium in front of the full attendance of town selectmen, parents, grandparents, and friends and other relatives. I could picture it, too.

The scene didn't have to appear as awful as they pictured. I could walk slowly, and the unequal leg size and foot twisted inward would appear less obvious. Though my foot was not straightening, I walked easier with the brace. My limp was less distinct.

With the weight I had lost by exercising more walking with the brace, my *pudge* was melting. Mama had to take in Hanne's hand-me-downs. Her clothes included a few stylish clothes that I could mix and match. Sometimes, I almost felt pretty in the outfits.

I took the school stairs only when I had to. I never went outside during lunch time. The building contained modern indoor plumbing with a water closet on both floors. Once I arrived on the second floor, I stayed until the end of the day.

Career dress looks for the slim lines and beautifully coiffed Gibson girls

In 1924 the Gibson Girl ideal of slim long-legged beauty held the popularity it had promoted for over two decades but had changed to show a more modern look.

The Gibson Girls were sentimental but down-to-earth, modern yet classic, beautiful but not overly made up like the worldly women the church warned us about. Pastors, elders, deacons, and Sunday School teachers warned us about trusting in outward beauty instead of in the Lord.

From the fashion magazines, Ebba and I saw and liked hairstyles and clothes. Mama adapted our clothes for the first Butterick patterns. With her stitching skills and those patterns, Mama sewed any idea we brought her. I felt prettier, but no one at school said anything complimentary to me. Whispers within my hearing mentioned my uneven limp.

Hanne, Ebba, and I also poured over *Tales of Romance* and *All-Story Magazine* in private. Some stories had kissing and more between couples who weren't even engaged! The women were a cross between the strong-voiced women who had worked for the vote and silent film stars like Lillian Gish and Mary Pickford. I had never been to a film.

The magazines helped me understand the lure of temptation. I had never thought about these experiences, products, and viewpoints. I led a very restricted life. The magazines created a yearning in me to see and experience more in the world.

OUR YOUNGER HORSE, Jenny, had aged well and pulled us anywhere. But she loved to come home. I sat in our low cart and drove Jenny to 122A. Usually then, I'd turn Jenny around, give her a slap, and she'd trot back to our farm. She was as smart as a dog, but more stubborn. Papa didn't allow me to drive Jenny to school because that was dangerous.

Jenny was easily startled, but I drove well with Jenny. I had no regular responsibilities with her, but some days I clumped to the barn to brush her beautiful hide and mane. Because Papa organized the barn, I entered it without worry of falling against mowers, cultivators, harrows, rakes, or any trailed implements. Papa was rich in equipment through auction purchases. He cared for his equipment and loaned to neighbors in need.

In that spring of my hope, I drove Jenny in the little governess cart. My parents allowed me to go to the end of Bailey Road, Reservoir Road, or to a store on 122A. It was a gorgeous day, gliding beneath the overhead treetops. The sunshine invigorated me.

I harnessed Jenny and hooked her to the cart. That day only Mama was home and worked in her main vegetable garden while Axel crawled nearby and studied whatever he found. Mama kept an eye on him.

Jenny was patient while being hitched to the cart. I knew how to do that task, but I didn't enjoy hitching her. It felt fine if Jenny stood nicely, but sometimes she tossed her head or stomped her feet impatiently.

Today, just with my gentle hands and lead rope as guide, Jenny moved in front of the cart. She had a breast collar and light harness, which included a nose band, brow band, cheek straps, half-cheek snaffle bit, crown piece, and a check rein attached by a buckle.

We all learned to follow a routine every time we hitched Jenny to the cart. When the back strap and crupper were attached, with the crupper below the tail root and all the hair in place, we put on the breast collar with the traces done. Then the driving reins strung through the saddle terrets, bit ends loose, and the buckled hand ends were looped and placed through the back strap. Following this, we removed the lead rope and put on the bridle. I fastened the driving reins to the bit, the throatlatch, and the noseband.

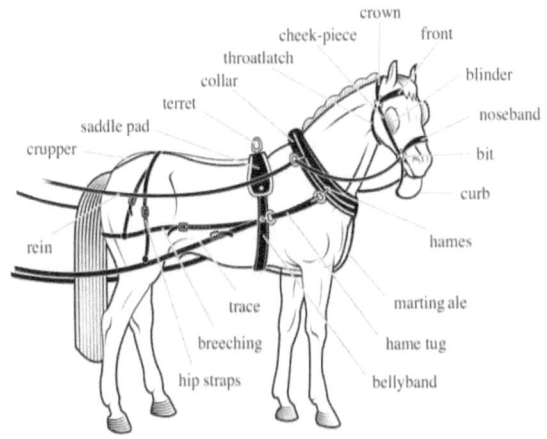

We were never to put the horse in the vehicle without the bridle on the animal. With the shafts lifted, even I could pull the light vehicle to the horse. I lowered them gently on each side. Then I guided the shafts to the loops. Since I was alone, I did the near side first and then moved to the off side. I was careful never to have the ends of the shaft forward of Jenny's shoulders. I fastened the traces, of the same length, then to each side with no slack. The tips of the shafts should never come beyond the shoulder or they could catch a horse behind the shoulder. That would be dangerous.

I wrapped traces over the shaft, around, underneath, and behind the shaft loop. Then I buckled on the outside of the trace. The process sounded complicated like a puzzle; I'd done the puzzle many times by heart. Last, I fastened the check rein.

It took great effort to hoist myself onto the seat, but I rose easier now because I was stronger and slimmer. I sat straight with my arms slightly extended and my elbows close to my body. I could see through the space between Jenny's ears. I held the reins lightly to keep verbal contact to remind her I was in control.

Papa had adjusted the seat and footboard for Mama, Ebba, and me. My feet lay apart to keep my balance with my good foot ahead of the twisted foot. I was an experienced driver with one or both hands. If anyone else came on the road, I used two hands.

Papa had told us pleasure came from driving a horse properly. Driving any vehicle was a big responsibility. I had gained confidence through the process and in the driving.

We were half way down Bailey Road when Jenny pulled to the right. A stone culvert ran underneath the road for a brook's path. Away from the road, it opened to the full brook. Many carriages stopped there for their animals to drink, so the animals and vehicles had formed a path.

I let Jenny drink. Pulling back on the reins, I guided her to a step down the slope and to the water's edge. It was easy to daydream as Jenny drank.

Jenny suddenly tossed her head as if nodding to someone. No one was there. Something, though, had happened to the check rein. Papa had drilled us we should never leave the reins unbuckled or one rein might drop. I had buckled everything. But the rein fell around her leg. If Jenny noticed the rein by her leg, she might rear, thinking it was a snake.

No one could see me from Bailey Road. I had to get off the cart, find and put the rein in place, and hopefully return to the cart and home without much difficulty. I took a deep breath and made the first move.

Jenny lifted her head, coughed, and then drank again. While she continued that routine, I made my way off the cart. I wobbled and bumped against her, startling her. She jumped away from me. I fell.

I lay on the ground, Jenny galloped away over the hill dragging the small cart behind her.

At the edge of the pond, myy skirts became soaked.

Immediately I lost the warmth and joy of the day. Once Jenny showed up in the yard without me, Mama and anyone else at home would worry, be filled with fear. They'd come looking for me.

I dragged myself back away from the water. Moving to the top of the hill seemed impossible. The soaked skirt and underskirt clung against my legs, I tripped. I rolled over. Anger and fear filled me. I hated my long and confining clothing. I sat in the sunlight and hugged my knees to my chest. The water sparkled, then looked slate blue with gray swirls.

The sunshine faded. My feet, legs, and skirt were soaked. Now would be a terrible time to get sick. I didn't want to catch pneumonia! *Oh, God! I need someone to find me,* I prayed.

The sun came from behind the clouds to encourage me. I would wait as calm and still as the pond. I just needed to think about something that would make me feel better. I thought about Mark Twain's writing about the crazy New England weather. He'd given a humorous speech about New England weather in New York City. I had memorized most weather sections of that speech for a speech contest at school. Maybe if I recited some it would take my mind off my fear and discomfort. Someone might hear me and come to help. Reciting loudly, I hoped I sounded unafraid yet wished desperately for rescue.

"I reverently believe that the Maker who made us all makes everything in New England but the weather. I don't know who makes that, but I think it must be raw apprentices in the weather-clerk's factory who experiment. In the spring I have counted one hundred and thirty-six different kinds of weather inside of four-and-twenty hours."

I paused in my loud delivery to glance at the road. No one. A nervous flutter grew in my chest. But I swallowed it and returned to the speech. I pretended I was speaking in front of a large group of people, hard of hearing people. I forced myself to speak louder while the sun disappeared again. In my heart I prayed someone would hear me, better people talk about The Joren's crazy daughter than the helpless crippled daughter. I continued reciting Mark Twain's words wishing for his wit to give me courage. I felt ready to cry.

"One of the brightest gems in the New England weather is the dazzling uncertainty of it. There is only one thing certain about it: you are certain there is going to be plenty of it—a perfect grand review; but you never can tell which end of the procession is going to move first. You fix up for the drought; you leave your umbrella in the house and sally out, and two to one you get drowned....Mind, in this speech I have been trying merely to do honor to the New England weather—no language could do it justice."

I loved good words. Words usually had the power to drive away my fears. Books had helped me hope many times. I might marry if I met a man who had a way with words like Mark Twain, Mr. Samuel Clemens.

My eyes searched in every direction. I saw no sign of anyone. The false courage that had temporarily distracted me through recitation faded. Chills sent me to shivering.

I faced the awful thought: No one was coming for me. No one had seen Jenny. Perhaps for the first time something distracted Jenny from returning home. If she did not go home, no one would have any idea I might be in trouble.

The sun was almost gone. Being chilled was always bad for me. The moistness in the breeze predicted rain. I'd be foolish to continue sitting and hugging my knees. Much as I might hate the thought, I needed to move even if I had to crawl. I hoped it wouldn't come to that supreme embarrassment.

With the multi-ring brace on, I moved up the hill. Rain fell straight as pins and cold. The ground was uneven making the brace painful against my skin. Step with the good left foot. Lift and drag the gimpy right one. In my slow hobble, I wondered if anyone who could walk thanked God for that ability.

I was exhausted and visibly trembling before I reached the top of the hillside path. Stopping, I looked for a sign of another person. I could just see the road. No one in sight in any direction. Why did I have to be reduced to the miserable helpless motions of a baby?

The one way to progress faster was the baby method. At my age, crawling was ignominious, but no other option was available if I was going to travel up the hill and down the road on my own. Someone would eventually see me and help me. Crawling in a long skirt and under slips essential to modesty was beyond ridiculous.

That vision seared my mind so vividly, I knew it was no longer an option for me. If I had to die of exposure, I was not going to crawl. I just couldn't face the neighbors seeing Adia and Asa's crippled daughter crawling up a hill or down the road. I'd rather die of a chill than have someone see me crawl. I sat beside the road and rested my forehead on my knees. I cried hard and didn't notice when the rain grew fiercer than my tears.

9

CAREER HOPES AND A CAR SALESMAN

"Doves should be caught in mid-air as they fly towards or past you. Once the bird has been caught, it must be handled correctly….handling should always be gentle and should not compress the chest in any way that may reduce breathing ability. Unlike mammals, birds do not breathe by physical exertion of the lungs….birds breathe by expanding the entire chest and abdomen to pump air in and out of an extensive network of air sacs found throughout the body cavity and hollow bones and then into the relatively immobile lungs.
Danny Brown, *A Guide to Pigeons, Doves, and Quail*

At the high school graduation ceremony, I gave the first speech. Being the top student entitled me to at least that honor. I walked as evenly as possible to the podium in the dress Mama had sewn from a special Butterick pattern. My dress was of fine silk blend fabric, the best in Holden. I felt successful and pretty and hoped no trace of disappointment showed in my demeanor because a young man was listed as Valedictorian. He was two full points behind my average in every subject. He was a dedicated student from an important family. His name and appearance inspired students' admiration and hope for the future graduates. He looked like he could be older than 20.

I knew I was not valedictorian because I was a cripple with an uncertain future from an undistinguished family. The program did not name me as Valedictorian and I had no special tassel. The school did not desire my image the future's inspiration. I did not appear more mature than my years. No one I knew aspired to be like me or my family except for some Christian friends who knew my parents loved God and served in the community.

During refreshment time, I received compliments. I smiled and thanked everyone politely. Several teachers could not meet my eyes at all during the graduation celebration. My parents glowed with pride. I did not tell them that I should have the title of Valedictorian. Only Ebba knew I should have been valedictorian.

After I graduated from high school, I entered the first wilderness time of my life. Each day seemed like wandering as the Israelites and looking for the place God had for me. My family had forgotten my day in the rain, though Papa insisted I never stop in the little carriage to let Jenny drink again. I would never forget my despair that day. The week following helpless feelings of discouragement assailed me while I lay in bed, sick.

Now I had graduated and felt lost. My sleep found me fighting with bedcovers through the night. Hanne told me that could be due to panic. Why would I panic? I had endless time and no responsibilities. She told me I probably felt panicked about my future. That made me angry. Why should she think *my* future would be any worse than hers?

Because she saw me as a cripple. Did the rest of my family

see me like that? Even when I inhaled slow deep breaths, I felt smothered. My bones seemed made of lead, and sometimes I could hardly move.

I wanted the people I loved to see me as whole person, not as a cripple. I wanted to show them I could do anything anyone with two strong legs could do, any activity that didn't require two strong legs. I wanted a career. I wanted to live free as a bird because I didn't want to depend on others to care for me.

Why couldn't people look beyond a wobbly shrunken leg and twisted foot? All my work best in Latin, English, French, mathematics, and history were for nothing if I couldn't continue on to a career because marriage seemed beyond my dreams.

A business career appealed to me. A business school must be located between Worcester, Framingham, and Boston. Telling Mama and Papa was difficult. I didn't want to see their exchange of expressions that said, *Our crippled child thinks she can leave us.*

A month after I graduated, Hanne left for Pennsylvania to live with Ingelise, Anthony, and Elenora. She missed Ingelise and said she wanted a life in a city. In our house on Bailey Road, I had the people who loved and believed in me: Mama, Papa, Ebba, and Axel.

I talked to Ebba about my plans for a career in business. We searched directories, magazines, and newspapers for a good business school. Over the next three months, we gathered information about business school programs.

If I truly had courage, I thought I should experience more than Worcester. Though Worcester did not have the fame of Boston, it was a large city and special to me as part of my home area. Still, I looked at a bigger city accessible by train, Boston.

As early as 1835, railroads were completed from Boston to Worcester, Lowell, and Providence. From these major cities, other routes to many smaller towns were connected. During World War I, service was curtailed on many Boston lines to conserve fuel, labor, and equipment. World War I time was a real turning point for the railroads. There had to be many cutbacks so materials could be put into the war effort.

Sadly, most items cut were never reinstated. By the time WWI was over, automobiles had captured the nation's imagination. Even Worcester had multiple car dealerships. Everyone dreamed of their own car, and railroad use spiraled down as cars became more common.

A car was not even a thought for me. If I equipped myself for a business occupation, secretary and then administrative assistant would make a career path. I would aim to become an executive secretary. Boston business schools, only fifty miles from Holden and Worcester, had many options. I would visit different schools and see their programs.

In the fall of 1924, Ebba agreed to take the train into Boston with me. Mama and Papa let her miss a school day for our visits to business schools. Mark Twain said, "I have never let schooling interfere with my education." My parents understood the truth in that humor.

I used my graduation gifts of money and my egg and flower money for our trips into Boston. I sold white and brown eggs and bouquets through two Holden town markets.

Ebba and I took an early train to Boston's North station. I went with high hopes. Traveling with Ebba, I thought I could overcome anything difficult in traveling. Ebba smoothly took my arm and we leaned against one another while walking.

The highlight of the first day was the city's appearance and atmosphere. On an ice-box crisp, autumn day, we saw the leaves' colors in the parks. We found our way around the city easily, though movement over curbs and steps was difficult for me. Ebba helped me overlook these and chattered a commentary distracting me from my physical dependence on her.

Naïve as a child, I hadn't considered Boston would have faster-paced and worse streets and sidewalks than Worcester. Every activity was harder. Ebba kept me from collapsing into tears. I wondered why they didn't design walk ways to gently slope to street level. Then anyone, even a mother pushing a baby buggy, could ease to higher or lower levels?

I had planned a meal each day in the city. On the first day after an unpleasant tour of a cramped secretarial school, Ebba and I walked to the Parker House Hotel, a famous hotel since before the Civil War. The hotel dining room took credit for culinary inventions such as Boston scrod, Parker House rolls, and Boston cream pie. Ebba and I tried all those dishes.

We were late for the afternoon appointment because walking took longer than estimated. I wondered how long the walk would be with ice and snow. I couldn't afford cabs to travel in a city. The administrator did not like waiting past the set time. Just from his sour face, he proclaimed, *"How can anyone expect to have a business career without arriving on time for an appointment?"*

When he glanced at me, his eyebrows lowered and his face glowered at my limp. He frowned deeply every time he looked at my twisted foot. I felt sick to my stomach by the tour's end and wondered if I could visit another school. I did do that with Ebba's supportive companionship.

Our second excursion into Boston was during a cold gray

day in late November. When the school staff noticed my pronounced limp and twisted foot, they seemed to think I was mentally deficient. They looked at me as if to say, *And how in the world did you think you might become a career girl, a well-trained secretary representing* **our** *school?*

The morning tour was cursory. I think they added steps and staircases to our tour just to make me struggle and to recognize my foolishness in hoping to become a professional secretary. They were dismissive and rude. I felt humiliated. I had never wanted Ebba to witness such demeaning treatment of me even though I had faced it for years.

To distract us, I splurged by taking a cab to the Oyster House Restaurant. The Oyster House was older than the Parker House. Famous people, such as Daniel Webster, had spent time in the Oyster House. Since 1826 the Oyster House has served a variety of seafood meals.

The Oyster House made as wonderful a distraction as the Parker House. We were treated politely and kindly. The service was excellent, and the food hot and delicious. I had scallops; Ebba, salmon. We each had a small cup of seafood chowder before our meals.

As we finished, I entertained Ebba with the story of Charles Foster from Maine. He had invented toothpicks and the idea of restaurants giving them to customers. He hired Harvard boys to enter the Oyster House to ask for toothpicks after their meals. Toothpicks caught on. Ebba and I laughed and soaked in the rich atmosphere before another school visit.

The afternoon school visit was as awful as the morning one. Staff at the school seemed insulted that I had even chosen to visit their school. They stared at my crippled foot and spoke to me as if I was mentally slow.

Ebba and I were quiet on the ride home. Once seated on

the train, we gave in to our exhaustion. I shut my eyes. Neither wanted to say the obvious. Boston was not an option for me. I would continue my plans elsewhere. I was smart enough to attend a Normal School, but a four-year education was more than I wanted.

Worcester was a big city in my backyard. I hadn't wanted to look at its business schools, but I would. I refused to relinquish my career dream and hope for independence. I had not crawled up all those steps at the Gale building to give up now!

Ebba knew when I was feeling low. On the train she held my hand for most of the return trip. Papa met us. He could tell from one look at us that the trip had been difficult. We didn't talk on the ride home.

Everyone avoided the business school topic throughout the winter of 1924. Only Axel was untouched by my sadness and frustration. He was delighted by everything he could discover in his constant investigations in the house, in the yard, and wherever we went.

Watching Axel grow soothed my spirit. He asked questions about everything. He built things out of wood and metal scraps. He ran and climbed and learned to ride a bike. He was my entertainment and the household's joy.

During the winter I stayed home and helped Mama with indoor tasks, freeing her for other projects such as visiting shut-ins and taking meals to those who were sick or unable to buy food they needed.

Ebba and I visited Nazarene Chapel in Worcester when the roads were clear. We knew our parents had gone there before they moved to Holden, and we felt curious to experience worship there. Papa let Ebba and me drive to Worcester in the little cart. What a wonderful surprise it was to see our former favorite teacher, Miss MacIntosh, now Mrs. Stanley

Washburn, entering the church just steps ahead of us. member at the Nazarene Chapel.

Mrs. Washburn, recognized us immediately. "Annelise, Ebba, how wonderful to see you two here. Are your parents coming too?"

"No. They said we could come to visit because we wanted to experience a church service where they first worshipped when they came to Worcester."

"My husband and I are members here. Please, come sit with us. He is just ahead there sitting with our children."

We followed her and slipped into the same row with her. Her husband sat on the far end of the row. Then their 3 children, then our dear teacher, and finally us. She handled her three little children easily. Her twins, boys were four, her daughter, two. They clung to each other and stared quietly at us.

The Nazarene Chapel was similar to Holden First Baptist Church, but with more pulpit-pounding and singing. I liked the liveliness of the service and the friendly people. Attending a church with just Ebba instead of my parents caused me to feel like an adult.

After the service Mrs. Washburn introduced us to others in the congregation including a Mr. James Burtin. He was visiting the Nazarene Chapel while spending time with his cousin, Enoch Burtin a friend of Mr. and Mrs. Washburn. James talked with equal animation to everyone.

He had just moved to Worcester and was a car salesman. I said that was a forward-looking job since cars would be the main future transportation. His light brown eyes sparkled at my comment.

After our next day's supper, I played the piano, Ebba helped Mama clean up, and Axel and Papa were in the barn. Someone knocked on the front door, loud enough for us to hear it over the piano. No one we knew used the front door. People usually came to the back door or the side entrance Papa had added a year after we moved to the farm.

Ebba went to the front door. She reappeared with James Burtin. Mama and I felt totally surprised and our expressions must have shown this. Ebba giggled. James looked slightly embarrassed.

"Good afternoon," His deep voice and a respectful tone as he looked and spoke to Mama.

Afternoon? I looked at Mama and Papa's wedding clock. They looked at the clock too and then back at this handsome young man who wore a suit, fine shoes, and a smile. It was before six o'clock, so the time was still technically afternoon.

"I'm James Burtin. I met your lovely daughters at the Nazarene Chapel yesterday, and I hope you don't mind that I came to call on them, Annelise in particular."

"No, not at all," Momma said through her surprise. "Have a seat, please, Mr. Burtin. You say you came to call on Annelise in particular. You are a direct man."

"I can be, Mrs. Joren. In my work I also need to know how to be indirect and patient. I prefer to be clear. I work as a salesman."

Just after James gave this answer, Papa and Axel came in through the side entrance.

"There's a car out front!" Axel said with delight.

I thought Papa had a slight frown as Axel made this observation and James smiled.

"That's my car. I work for Bland Motors in Worcester."

"You are a young man of the modern world." Papa's observation did not sound like a compliment.

Mid-1920s Pontiac

"Would you like a cup of tea and some oatmeal cookies? Have you had dinner? We just cleared away our supper." Mama offered a warmer tone and hospitality.

"Actually, I left right after work. Mrs. Washburn gave me directions. I guess she was a teacher to your girls."

"Yes. In their elementary years, and she was one of their favorites. Sit at the table, Mr. Burtin. I will reheat some food for you. It won't take long."

"I don't want to be a bother, Mrs. Joren," he added.

"It's no trouble. Have a seat."

Ebba and I cleared the dress patterns from the table. Ebba and Mama had planned to work on creating some warm clothing. Ebba kept darting glances at me and smiling as to say, *Good for you, Annelise! You impressed a good-looking man,* but we didn't say anything aloud. We listened as Mama and James Burtin conversed.

When Mama set roast pork, carrots, and biscuits in front of James Burtin, Axel walked up to him and asked, "What is your name sir?" He gazed at the stranger.

"I'm James Burtin. And who are you?" James stood and offered his hand to Axel. They shook hands.

"I'm Axel Joren." Axel thought shaking hands with a grown-up was fun.

James stood until Papa told him to sit and finish the meal Mama had put in front of him. By the time James had finished, conversation seemed easy between him, Mama, and Papa. Ebba and I sat quietly. Axel sat on Papa's knee.

Coming to visit a home and naming the young lady a gentleman wanted to visit stood as common courtesy when a man was interested in courting. Ebba and I had not imagined having such a caller as we were both younger than eighteen. I knew people thought I looked older than eighteen. What would Papa say? I could see the seemed to suddenly frown.

Outside evening had fallen. No streetlights alleviated the darkness near our farm. Papa cleared his throat and said, "Our daughters are very bright young ladies, James, but they are young. Annelise was a top student and should have, in my estimation, been Valedictorian." Hearing Papa speak about my graduation was the first time I realized he and Mama knew I had been denied valedictorian.

Papa continued, "Annelise went through high school in three years and rushed through her elementary years and was young when she entered high school. Annelise is looking for the right business school now to further her education. She won't be eighteen until the end of the summer. Ebba just started high school."

Jim Burtin seemed very surprised. Ebba and I looked at one another as we realized James had not asked Mrs. Washburn our ages. "I see, sir. I thought they were older. Mrs. Washburn wasn't correct in her estimate of their ages."

"They can seem older."

"Yes, sir." James glanced at Ebba and me and sighed. "Well, I best be heading back to town. Thank you for the wonderful dinner, Mrs. Joren. I didn't expect anything like a home-cooked meal. It was a treat. Annelise and Ebba, I am glad to know more about you and your family, you especially Axel.

You seem like a friendly and smart young man. Mr. and Mrs. Joren, thank you for your hospitality this evening."

"You're welcome," Papa said. "If you're out this way, feel free to visit. We're far enough off the main road that we have few changes in our daily routines. Aida always has plenty of food. You would be welcome." Papa was sincere, but the invitation was to visit the family, not to spend time with one daughter. He and Axel walked James to the front door. They watched him leave from there. We watched from the windows. Axel exclaimed in delight when James started the car engine and the headlights illuminated the road.

When James drove out of sight I went back to the piano. Mama went to the sewing, and Ebba completed another round of cleaning up. Papa sat back in his favorite chair and Axel climbed into his lap with a book. Papa liked to read to Axel before he put his son to bed.

Mama said, "Girls, you didn't tell us about impressing a young man when you visited Mrs. Washburn's church."

"We didn't know." I didn't want my parents to think Ebba or I would hide the fact.

"He seemed like a fine young man. Oxford is a good town. Car selling, though—well that's modern," Papa said as he sat in his favorite chair and picked up his paper.

"But he was at a Nazarene Chapel, Asa. I think a young person today can have a modern career if he is anchored in good values." Mama was quickly supportive of Ebba and me and our hopes. She was strict in her expectations, but she had love in her heart and in the daily prayers for us.

"I agree." Papa said in a pensive tone. I wondered if Papa really believed a modern young man could have good values. After all, James didn't regularly attend the Nazarene Chapel. He had only been a visitor there this Sunday.

10

BUSINESS SCHOOL AND A BEAU?

"Seven musts for dove raising are, a dry house with protection from rain and snow, separate houses for mated pairs and odd birds, a cozy flypen that dries out easily, suitable feed ration free from contamination, suitable mineral ration free from contamination, water suitable for human consumption and protected from contamination, suitable material for building a nest. If any one of these seven is neglected, trouble of some sort will eventually occur." **W.E. Levi, *Encyclopedia of Pigeon Breeds***

How often we can miss the good that is close by taking it for granted and focusing on faraway places. I felt like a fool when I looked at Worcester business schools. Three or four had been in business over a decade, and a couple had good records of helping their graduates find good jobs. I could have saved time and money by looking at Worcester schools first.

L.G. Fairchild's Office School, located in the State Mutual building downtown, offered the most options for business training. Mr. Fairchild started his school as the Phoenix Commercial Institute with training classes in the Graphic Arts building on Foster Street. The school grew in courses and students. Mr. Fairchild had a good reputation, and the investors changed the name to reflect his leadership.

Courses were offered in multi-graphing, stenography, promotional mailings, listings and categorical divisions, copying, typewriting, mimeographing, indexing/cataloging, direct mailings/circulars, ediphone, dictaphone transcription, shorthand, invoicing and payrolls, commercial law, arithmetic, accounting, spelling, punctuation, and penmanship. Not only were the informative and skill courses more than adequate, Mr. Fairchild's philosophy added to the school for professionalism in attitude and practices.

He believed, "Education is from within." He also said about the school, "Our individual training plan gives each student the fullest value in rapid progress."

I soon saw why Mr. Fairchild compared service to gold. He believed that as valuable gold is worked into intricate designs, an office worker's worth is dependent on the value of service and measured by her professionalism when handling intricate challenges. One's measure, he said, was taken by how well one lived life. That included how well a person did in effort, planning, thoughtfulness, and anything that would be a positive reputation. .

The price of courses I could afford, and I would live at home and commute to Worcester each day. Papa drove to a mechanic job in Worcester at eight each morning. I could ride with him. When his work day finished, he would stop and pick me up at the school. Knowing him, I guessed he would have many questions for me each day about what I had learned or had to practice.

School hours would not run from eight to four, Papa's

work hours, but while I waited for him, I could do my assignments and read. I loved to read. Sometimes I felt if someone told me I could not read, that person might as well say I could not breathe. Reading and music were my luxuries and necessities.

Mr. Fairchild and his wife interviewed me. I wore one of my simple but stylish outfits and Ebba fixed my hair in a business chignon with a loose curl in front of my ears and at each temple. Mr. and Mrs. Fairchild told me my career choice of a professional secretary was wise. I could become skilled and efficient without much walking in my day. I liked that the staff who, like the Fairchild's. took my disability into consideration as if it was only a practical matter. Their comments on my personal appearance in written summaries said, *pleasant* and *very presentable*.

I passed high on the written application test. They said I needed no penmanship, spelling, or arithmetic courses. I scored perfectly in those areas. I did need accounting and the full variety of the business classes that would give me skills and procedures essential for success.

The school was small with only a half dozen classrooms for multiple courses all day. The building had an elevator, another mark of a different future from the past. I could see it would be easy for me to move from class to class. Pursuing my dream and moving in a professional world felt exhilarating, almost unbelievable.

Worcester had many first and earliest models of mechanical conveniences. Compared to Boston, Worcester was low-keyed, but a good city with the advances of any major city. In 1878 Charles Hill Morgan patented a direct-action hydraulic elevator and installed the first type in the Washburn & Moer Wire Works in Worcester.

The Commerce building, Worcester's first skyscraper,

connected two buildings with bridges on floors three through nine. The main building, built in 1896, added continual improvements since WWI. It had four elevators.

Mama and Papa were relieved I had found something close to home. Ebba told me she had prayed I might find something close to home so we could continue to have time together in evenings. Axel told me when he got older, he would drive me to my classes and one day he would have a car.

The pace and values of the new world—so different from my family's world—left me in a turmoil. How quiet and remote Bailey Road was compared to downtown Worcester. Trolleys, cabs, carriages, and cars filled the Worcester streets.

Papa enjoyed the extra time with me during our commute, and I quickly saw I was correct in guessing Papa would ask many questions about my classes. He asked questions about Mr. Fairchild's ideas concerning the psychological principles of education applied to business training. Papa surprised me with what he knew. He was good with building and repairing, farming, raising animals, running a household, and handling personal business. I didn't often hear his thoughts on other topics.

I had guessed my love of reading came from Mama. Both Mama and Papa read. Primarily they read and studied the Bible.

The summer weather was glorious, and I liked to read outside when I had enough time between classes. I found an outside bench near flower beds the Worcester Garden Club planted and maintained. I enjoyed the sunshine and read until one week day when a shadow fell across me. The day had full sunshine so I looked up immediately to see what had blocked that light from me. There stood James Burtin.

"Why Mr. Burtin, what a surprise!"

"I'm glad to see you haven't forgotten me. May I sit beside you?"

"Of course," I said as I wondered how my business outfit appeared to him: casual white blouse, colorful cotton paisley vest, plain skirt and shoes, and a draw string bag large enough for everything I might need during a day.

"You look lovely, Annelise, older than your age. Are you eighteen now?"

"I will turn eighteen on August twenty-eight."

"Does your family have birthday parties?"

"Not full-fledged parties. We serve the birthday person's favorites at supper with cake and sometimes ice cream. Ebba is good at churning ice cream. I ask for that on my birthday."

"And you are on this bench because you are taking secretarial classes nearby?"

"Yes. I'm in the Fairchild Office School. It's been great. They are more personable and kind than any people I met at Boston business schools. They also have a wonderful record of graduates' employment. They have letters of appreciation from employers thrilled with their secretaries."

"Sounds good. Are you on a break?"

"Yes. I had an 8 a.m. class, invoices and payrolls. Then stenography, then a break. Then accounting, lunch, cataloging and indexing. In the fall the school days will run longer."

"Then you finish at . . ."

"At two. I do assignments or read until Papa picks me up at four. I ride in and home with Papa. He has a job as a mechanic at working on the elevator invention. His company wants to be as respected as Otis."

"I'm happy you found a school close to home."

"Thank you," I replied.

"And how long do you have for your lunch break?"

"An hour. I bring my lunch most days, though I know Worcester has some lovely eateries, bakeries, and restaurants."

"I come this way often on business. Annelise, would you have lunch with me sometime?"

"I suppose . . ."

"How about tomorrow?"

"I . . . I." I was flustered. He'd caught me off-guard. He was charming in voice and manners. I found it hard to believe he wanted to spend time with me.

"Annelise, look across the street. Do you see the Foster Dining Room?"

"Yes."

"I've had lunches there with clients of the dealership. It serves delicious food in quick time. We could have lunch there tomorrow."

I told myself lots of girls were married before they were eighteen, girls dumber and smarter than I. They must have accepted dates before they decided on marriage. Why should I be shy about saying yes? These were modern times. I needed to experience more of life. Mama and Papa wouldn't expect me to ask their permission in everything.

"I'd love to, Mr. Burtin."

"Great. And I'd appreciate it if you'd call me James. When you say Mr. Burtin, I look around to see if my father is standing behind me."

"All right, James," I said with a smile. "I will see you here tomorrow at noon."

"Thank you. I am glad I walked this way today. I've thought of you the past months, but I wanted to show up on your doorstep again when you were at least eighteen."

"I guess downtown Worcester is open to any age."

"I guess so."

He stood, so I did. He reached out with his left hand, making my heart flutter as I thought he would take my hand.

Instead, he turned my book to read the binding. "*Historical Collections of Massachusetts.* Hmmm, not what I'd call light reading." He kept his hand on the book. My hand was also on the book. We were almost touching.

"I love to read, and I love history," I told him. "It's interesting to learn about the place and people who formed this city that has affected my life."

"You don't sound like any seventeen-year-old I have conversed with, Miss Annelise Joren."

"Is that a compliment?"

"It definitely is. I must hurry on with my errands. I will meet you tomorrow, at noon, in front of the Mutual Building. We will cross the road together. You won't be in trouble for going to lunch with me, will you?"

"I don't think so."

"You'll take the chance?"

"I will, and thank you for the invitation."

"You're welcome. I look forward to tomorrow." He tipped his summer straw hat before he walked away, energetic and jaunty.

Oh, my! My pulse raced. How would I concentrate the rest of this day? What would I say on the ride home? What would I tell Mama? I'd tell Ebba everything. She would be happy for me. She thought Mr. Burtin had nice eyes and a lovely smile.

Ebba wondered, why did Mama and Papa use our ages to tell him not to return soon? I didn't know the answer. That was not a pleasant realization.

～

THAT EVENING, when I told Ebba everything about my conversation with James. she was excited for me. I thought she might have a crush on James Burtin. She admitted she could like someone like him, but he was too old for her. We agreed there was no reason to keep secrets from Mama and Papa. At dinner I broached the subject slowly.

"I had an interesting meeting today," I started. "I sat on the bench outside the Mutual building, reading, and Mr. James Burtin came by. He was doing work errands and took a few minutes to talk."

"That is a surprise," Mama said after a quick glance at Papa.

"He asked me about my secretarial training. When he learned I had an hour for lunch, he asked me to meet him for lunch tomorrow. I told him I usually brought a lunch, but he wants to take me to Foster's across the street. People have quick meals there, or so he said."

A lull fell as the mashed potatoes passed from Mama to Papa. "And what did you tell Mr. Burtin?" Papa asked softly. I couldn't tell if he was upset or angry. He just sounded calm.

"At first, I was tongue-tied. It was such a surprise. I felt . . . flattered. Then I thought since it was an invitation to a simple lunch in the open that it would be all right. I said yes."

"Thank you for telling us, Annelise," Mama spoke quickly. Papa was quiet and had a frown. "You know how Ingelise's secretive actions broke our hearts, and even Hanne's leaving, after making plans with Ingelise, was upsetting. You're a good girl to tell us all these parts of your day and decisions. You know Papa and I entrust you to the Lord daily. He is the only one who can watch over you and be with you all the time."

"Annelise and Ebba are good sisters," Axel said with

confidence. He had only had one visit with Hanne, and had never met his eldest sister.

"They are, indeed," Mama agreed, "and Hanne and Inge-lise would be good sisters to you too, but they live far away. I don't know when we'll see them."

"I like Annelise and Ebba fine," he added.

"Thank you, Axel. We like you, too. We thought we'd never have a little brother, and then there you were." Ebba's eyes sparkled whenever she talked with Axel. I was sure she'd be a wonderful mother for her own children.

"I agree with Ebba, Axel," I told him. "You are a wonderful little brother. Ingelise and Hanne don't realize the good times they miss."

Axel smiled and dug into his seconds. He usually ate double portions, but he ran, climbed, hiked, and rode a bike. He was not pudgy.

"I hope you will continue to be open with us, Annelise. We know you will make your own decisions. Your father and I are always concerned to protect you."

"I know, Mama. I'm glad you're not upset. I promise to be proper during lunch tomorrow with Mr. Burtin."

"That's wise, Annelise. Remember Ben Franklin's saying, 'Glass, china, and reputations are easily cracked and never well mended.'" Papa said that before he lapsed into silence for the rest of the meal.

Mama and Ebba were quiet. Only Axel chattered between mouthfuls until he asked, "May I be excused?"

The conversation had gone well. I wanted to be honest with my parents. I had seen their wounds from Ingelise's secrecy and decision to marry Anthony, then Hanne scooting off to Pennsylvania. Hanne had a serious beau too. She'd just recently told Ebba in a letter.

Almost every evening we had a family devotional time

before Axel went to bed. We gathered in the kitchen, always warmer and filled with good scents. Papa took the big family Bible, and if we weren't reading through the Bible, which we did every other year, he chose a scripture passage to read to us.

Once Axel knew how to read, Papa assigned Axel the responsibility of looking up the chosen passage in the Bible. Ebba and I had taught Axel the books of the Bible. He found looking up passages easily and faster than Ebba or I could.

"Tonight, Axel, find Deuteronomy. Let's just review some basics. Find Deuteronomy, chapter five. I'll start reading, and we can all take turns. I'll read the long beginning portion," Papa said and read verses one through six.

We sat around the table for this family time of devotional worship. Papa could call on any of us to read. He would slide the big leather-covered Bible to the next person.

"Ebba, you read the next six verses," Papa said as he turned the Bible toward her.

In her gentle but firm voice Ebba read, "You shall have no other gods before me. You shall not make any graven image, or any likeness of anything that is in heaven above, or that is in the earth beneath, or that is in the waters beneath the earth: You shall not bow down unto them, nor serve them."

Papa took the Bible from Ebba and passed it to Axel.

Papa said, "The next part is about keeping the Sabbath. Your mother does a wonderful job of that by doing her work on Saturday, so only the essentials are done on the Sabbath. We have our pleasant Sabbath days because of a godly woman, like the wonderful woman described in Proverbs 31. Axel, you read the next three verses."

The Bible was passed to Axel, and he read with a little stumbling, "Six days you shall labor, and do all your work:

But the seventh day is the Sabbath of the LORD your God: in it you shall not do any work–"

Now Axel, pass the Bible to Annelise. Axel did this in his usual quick motion.

"Annelise, start at verse sixteen of chapter 5 and read to the end of the commandments."

I began to read. "Honor your father and your mother, as the LORD thy God has commanded; that your days may be prolonged, and that it may go well with you, in the land which the LORD thy God gives you. You shall not kill. Neither shall you commit adultery. Neither shall you steal. Neither shall you bear false witness against your neighbor. Neither shall you desire thy neighbor's wife, neither shall you covet your neighbor's house, his field, or his manservant, or his maidservant, his animals, or anything that is your neighbor's."

My fingertips felt scalded as I passed the Bible to Papa. He had me start reading with honor your father and mother and concluded after a warning about being envious. How did he know I struggled with envy? I would not want to admit it, but envy filled my mind and heart every day. I envied those who could walk and run. I envied who could travel long distances without being stared at or ignored. I envied the gracefulness and confidence of young women. Envy lived in me, but I hadn't told anyone.

Then Papa's deep voice read Deuteronomy, Chapter 5: 22-33. "These words the LORD spoke unto all your assembly in the mount out of the midst of the fire, of the cloud, and of the thick darkness, with a great voice: and he added no more. And he wrote them in two tables of stone, and delivered them unto me....You shall walk in all the ways which the LORD your God hath commanded you, that you may live, and that it may be well with you, and that you may prolong your days in the land which you shall possess."

When Papa finished, he closed the Bible, and we sat in silence, meditating. I wondered if anyone else thought his choices for us were deliberate.

Then Papa said, "Let us pray."

Each of us took a turn giving thanks. Then we went around, each giving praise. Papa required us to give thanks and praise to God each day. Then he required we look into our lives and speak words of repentance for something we had done or hadn't done. We learned early the difference between sins of commission and omission. Ebba and I usually chose to pray about an omission. We thought it easier to be honest about something we could have done but did not do.

Dear young Axel always blurted out a true situation, "Forgive me, Lord, for pulling Bessie's tail to make her run," or "Forgive me, Lord, for doing a lazy job cleaning the stalls." He was an honest boy, refreshing as a clear mountain stream.

In the final turns that we took around our family devotional time, we could God for something. Axel learned honesty and openness in prayer from our parents. They both prayed what was on their hearts, and they prayed for us, they expressed their concerns about our future lives and choices.

This night I was careful what I said. God knew my heart. My parents listened carefully to every word and to my tone. I prayed, "Heavenly Father, please give me wisdom in making choices for my future." That was as careful and honest as I could be then.

11

COMPETITION AND CHURNING

"Doves, like all birds, have specific care needs that must be met over the years they will live." **Kind Planet Humane Education on Dove Care**

James Burtin seemed like the beau I'd dreamed of right from the time of our first luncheon. I did my best not to show that my heart and stomach did somersaults whenever I saw James. During our first lunch together, I knew James could tell I felt awkward. This experience of having a lunch with a young man had never been mine. What could we discuss?

"I have noticed, Annelise, that you like stories and history. I do too. Your family lives in Holden but you told me you were born in Worcester. Have you learned about Worcester history?"

"I have, and I remember quite a bit."

"Let's see. We can make it like a game while we wait for our meals to arrive. Which of us can come up with more or surprising facts. Would you enjoy that?"

In minutes, our exchange of information did become a game. Good-hearted competition undergirded our facts about Worcester. He was older, much more experienced in life and business than I was, intelligent. I don't think he realized how much I could know about the community just by reading. Nor did he or many people realize how easily I could memorize facts. We took turns giving facts about the city. It seemed an easy game. James showed surprise that I kept pace with him.

"In 1776," I told James, "Isaiah Thomas first publicly read the Declaration of Independence in Worcester." I went on to inform James that Mr. Thomas had printed the first U.S. dictionary in Worcester in the 18th century. He also printed the largest newspaper of the time, the *Massachusetts Spy*.

James knew Loring Coes of Worcester's Coes Knife Company had invented the monkey wrench.

I kept on with, "Charles Thurber, a Worcester resident, had patented the first modern-day typewriter."

James countered with Candy Cummings threw the first curveball pitch in Worcester in 1867 while playing for the Brooklyn Stars, and that curveball was a strike.

"The first national convention for women's suffrage was held in Worcester in October of 1850," I informed him.

James added, "Candlepin bowling was first developed in Worcester."

"A Worcester physician, Dr. R.L. Hawes, invented the first machine for folding plain paper into envelopes."

James knew that J. Lee Richmond of Worcester pitched the first perfect game in major league baseball history on June 12, 1880.

"Joshua Stoddard of Worcester had invented the steam calliope," I added.

"Dr. Robert H. Goddard of Worcester's Polytechnic Institute and Clark University had patented the first liquid fueled rocket in 1914," James told me.

We had fun with our odd facts tossed back and forth like a game of catch all the way through our lunch time. The hour passed quickly. I felt alive when I returned to classes.

On the ride home with Papa, I said little. He asked about the luncheon. I said the food was delicious, but I emphasized what a gentleman James Burtin had been. Papa didn't say much else.

At our second lunch James told me about his family and asked questions about mine. Ingelise's story shocked him because it had happened to a quiet, conservative, Protestant family. Yet he believed the eldest children were often path makers and tradition keepers or breakers, no in-between in his opinion.

James was a middle child who had become the eldest because his older brother had been killed in WWI. He had a much younger sister, as young to him as Axel was to me.

James asked at our third luncheon what kind of office I'd like to work in. "What are your career dreams?"

I gathered my courage and told him I hoped to have a job that would allow me to have my own home, even if it was a small apartment. He smiled.

Then he told me his hopes and plans. He didn't mention marriage. That surprised me. I certainly wasn't going to mention that. The conversation flowed, and he always complimented me on something I did or wore before I returned to work.

After that luncheon, I was disappointed to learn that he wouldn't see me until my birthday. He said he was busy and probably would not see me until my birthday dinner. Ebba assured me of her belief that James, polite and considerate, tried to avoid becoming too emotionally attached too early in the relationship.

Although I remembered smiling and chatting easily at that last shared lunch, I wondered right away if I had said or done something to offend James. I was more than a week until my birthday. What if he never saw me again except in passing on some down town street?

I felt nervous about his coming to my birthday dinner. I worried he might not show up when everyone knew he had told me he would come to my birthday celebration. The birthday loomed as a possible delight or misery. The actual day was a Saturday, and being home all that day, I thought more about him.

James arrived at 5:30. He received a warm welcome except from Papa who wasn't rude, just reserved. Papa was watchful, and James, careful. I could tell James deliberately chose his words thoughtfully with each question asked or answered. I called him Mr. Burtin in front of my family. Only Ebba knew I also called him James.

Ebba gave me a pair of exquisite black leather gloves for a present. Axel gave me perfume and said Ebba had helped him pick it out. Ingelise sent me $5 in a card, and Hanne did the same. Five dollars was a small fortune as a gift.

If I ponder how much $5 bought in 1925, I am amazed. I could buy a week's worth of food for my family. I didn't have to buy food because we lived off our land and what Papa and Mama bought. With $5, I could buy a dress and shoes. Every year prices rose, but what Ingelise and Hanne sent always increased. They sent money until I earned my own wages.

Papa and Mama gave me a beautiful evergreen-color wool coat lined with satin of the same color. I could slide the coat on and off easily. From its weight, I could tell the coat would be warm even on the worst winter days.

James gave me a Scottish-plaid scarf and a matching hat, a Scottish tam o'shanter. The beige background had a stripe of navy blue, black, yellow, and the coat's evergreen color.

"Your mother told me," James said, "the color of the coat through a note to me at the dealership. I wanted something to complete your business outfit." His thoughtfulness impressed the family. James had bought the items—made in Scotland—in a New York City store on a business trip.

We had my birthday cake frosted with my favorite buttery frosting that Mama made. Then we had ice cream Ebba had churned. The ice cream was so cold it made my throat ache. Inside I felt a real ache deep in my spirit with unshed tears over withheld emotions. I didn't know why I felt sad after a beautiful birthday dinner.

Maybe turning eighteen or having James with me and my family caused this strange churning in my emotions. My feelings had an agitation more active than Ebba's motions making ice cream. James, I wasn't his focus of attention.

James seemed to have an attraction for my whole family. At times his eyes lingered on Ebba's sweet face. In the next minutes he exchanged an invention idea with Axel, complimented my mother on her baking. Then he asked my father about a mechanical device. Was he acting to calm my parents' concern about his ardor?

Ardor—perhaps that overstated his feelings. The closest action to ardor appeared when James held my arm in his as we crossed Suburban Road to Foster's Dining Room. Did he feel more than a gentle attraction for me? I didn't have girlfriends to compare notes about relationships with young men. I only had Ebba as my sounding board. Every conversation with James seemed uncharted territory.

Throughout the evening I smiled and kept watching how James interacted with my family. He related well to everyone. James Burtin stayed through evening devotions. Papa finally started to look impressed at that point. I think Papa expected James would make excuses to leave before we started devotions.

Axel was supposed to read from Ephesians. When Axel could not find the book of Ephesians in the cluster of smaller books in the New Testament, James whispered, "Remember *General Electric Power Company.* That's the order for *Galatians, Ephesians, Philippians, Colossians.*"

Mama had James say the pattern out loud so we could clearly hear his trick for remembering. Laughter and approval greeted James's mnemonic trick.

Papa read chapter one of Ephesians. Before he read, he told us the apostle Paul, the chapter's author, had faced many difficulties and life-threatening situations. He had a physical problem that troubled him all the time, and yet he continued to do amazing things for the Lord. I realized Papa told me this to try to affirm my abilities and value.

Papa often had told me I had faced great trials with my physical limitation, but I could go forward like the apostle Paul. Though he didn't have to, Papa explained to James that he prayed for each of his children daily. He prayed for us to feel God's presence and guidance and to choose a life pleasing to God. James listened attentively. He seemed pleased to learn about our family time.

Papa then read scripture from chapter one of Ephesians where Paul said, "I also, after I heard of your faith in the Lord Jesus, and love unto all the saints. I cease not to give thanks for you, making mention of you in my prayers; That the God of our Lord Jesus Christ, the Father of glory, may give unto you the spirit of wisdom and revelation in the knowledge of him: The eyes of your understanding being enlightened."

Papa closed the Bible and added, "God will give you each

the fullness of life if you will trust Him with your lives and futures."

We bowed our heads. That night, because James was present, we didn't kneel beside our chairs. Papa prayed a short prayer. Some people in our church thought their responsibility was to pray at least fifteen or twenty minutes. Papa was not one of them.

James thanked us for allowing him to join our special family time. He shook hands with each before he left. Ebba said his hand lingered in my hand, but I wasn't sure. I thought only *He's holding my hand.* His hand was cool and dry. I expected a sweaty palm. I wondered when I would feel passion. I only had romantic ideas and hopes.

We watched him drive away.

"Are you and Ebba going to the Nazarene Chapel in Worcester tomorrow to worship with James?" Mama asked as she sent Axel to bed. Though Papa had the newspaper in front of his face, I knew he listened for my answer.

"Oh, no. We'll go with you and Papa. I think it is good when our whole family goes together to the Baptist Church. After all, that has been our family church in all the time we've lived in Holden." I smiled, gathered my presents, and went upstairs.

"Let me help you carry those," Ebba said. Her expression was quizzical. I could tell she was surprised at my decision.

I was surprised, too, but I didn't care if I saw James the next day. My confused and flustered feelings needed a separation from Mr. James Burtin. I wasn't sure what I needed beyond a break from the pressure of having him nearby. I could feel my family's concern that James could be the one and only beau for me, the only man who might marry me.

What did I need in a future husband? Someone who settled for a me? Someone who liked my family as much as me? Someone kind and polite rather than passionately in love with me, disability and all?

At several points in the evening, I had imagined talking over all the conversation and actions with Ebba. She had a fascination with Mr. Burtin. I knew she had sincere happiness for me to have a beau. Ebba could not be any kinder or sweeter a younger sister. Yet now I had no desire to rehash the evening with Ebba. What if I had made a terrible mistake? My head and heart hurt. I had no clear vision of a future with James.

WHOSE VALENTINE?

"Doves in particular have very fine and soft skin. This makes them prone to considerable damage from what would otherwise be a minor injury." **Danny Brown, *A Guide to Pigeons, Doves, and Quail***

In 1847 Esther Howland mass-produced the first commercial valentine in Worcester. I thought about this when I received a valentine from James in the mail. I opened the large, thick card without guessing what it could be; I had never received a valentine except from Ebba, a homemade one.

"A valentine! How beautiful!" Ebba gushed as she ran to look at the card. Mama came to look at the card too. They read the message, which seemed to me more friendly than sentimental, and the signature was a full name, definitely formal, James Burtin.

James had been coming to our house twice a month. I thought it was as much because he enjoyed family time and home cooking as that he cared for me. Twice a month he also asked me to lunch. I enjoyed having a beau, but I wondered if he knew how he really felt about me. My feelings still whirled in confusion about his calm easy friendship.

No one at the secretarial school knew how platonic our relationship was. They knew James had a good job, a pleasant manner, and good looks. What more could a girl want? My office thought James seemed wonderful for me.

Though Ingelise and I had little in common over the years, I thought the love she had for Anthony Trombino must have been a passionate and all-consuming love that was more important to a relationship than pretty valentines, family devotional times, and regularly scheduled luncheons and suppers.

Before the valentine arrived, I had been thinking it might be time to break from James. The beautiful valentine changed that thought, influencing me to at least let things go on. Perhaps James was deliberately slow in showing his affection because he wanted me to graduate and have a career before I settled down as a wife.

Ebba told me he was fine and sweet. She reminded me that I never had felt in a rush to marry. Fortunately, if a young woman was a secretary and married, she didn't have to give up employment until she was pregnant enough for others to see her condition.

When I was honest with myself, I didn't know if I wanted to be married. Then I wondered how I could even think of turning down a marriage opportunity with a kind, handsome, Christian, smart, career-oriented man.

The contrast between my dreams and my reality was sometimes too glaring to endure without tears. But no one else saw the tears. I held my tears for when I was alone. Not even Ebba saw them. I felt like a fool for wishing to be swept into a passionate romance.

~

IN SPRING, Papa worked full-time in Worcester. No cutbacks in the company had come though people predicted them. Worcester contained an odd mix of big companies, mills, and small new companies. Papa made good wages now because of his advanced mechanical skills. Because of his many skills with metal, wood, designing, and just great observation skills, Papa could solve problems that stumped other experienced farmers and craftsmen. We had all we needed and enough to share with others, who had less.

The country seemed to do well economically, but Papa made disturbing predictions for the decade's end. He had a feeling the country would face serious problems in 1929 or 1930. Companies, he said, spent money foolishly.

I wondered why a farmer-mechanic in a small New England town would think he had a grasp on the nation's economic future. Papa read many newspapers and had friends in varied businesses. Some people were single-minded with few interests and predictable patterns. These same characteristics emerged in Axel.

Papa and Axel spent much time together. I'd heard that as folks grew older, sleeping habits made sharing a room difficult. Papa snored loudly and slept some nights on the back porch with Axel. Those two could sleep through a lightning storm or blizzard's winds. Though the porch had a roof and windows and doors, it was not air-tight. On some mornings, frost lay on their heavily filled down covers. How they both scooted to stir the fire those mornings!

Mama was delighted to watch her loved ones enjoy each another's company. She loved us and bathed us daily in prayer for safety and wisdom. I used to wonder if other mothers prayed for their children as much. First Thessalonians says we should pray without ceasing. Mama did. While she kneaded bread, she talked to the Lord. While she worked in the garden, while she traveled around town leaving meals for families, while she did laundry, sewing, knitting, played the piano, she talked to the Lord.

Rarely, Mama vented her emotions with laughter. Usually, a surprise produced her laughs. One night when Axel bathed in the big tin tub near the single kitchen window that overlooked the backyard and the woodstove was casting wave after wave of heat, Papa, Mama, and I were all dozing in the warmth. Ebba had gone out to check on a new lamb in the barn.

When Ebba returned to the house and stepped on the porch, she scraped her nails across the window making a sound like a sharp claw on the glass. Axel heard the noise and yelled. The little fellow stood right up in the tub, pointed at the window, and shouted, "A robber! A monster! A wolf!"

Papa leapt to his feet, started toward the window, then looked back at his naked dripping wet son. Papa laughed. Ebba came inside, laughing so hard she could not speak. Mama and I laughed too, though not as hard as Papa and Ebba.

Even Axel laughed as he sank back down into the warm soapy water. We were all happy that evening. Quiet evenings together and laughter created a unity I should remember forever. Could I really look forward to moving out of this home?

Yes. I didn't want to be the spinster daughter at home. Why did I think I would stay unmarried? In my heart it was intuitive knowledge. If I could have a career and independence, that would fulfill a dream.

Finding a man to love me beyond my infirmities and moods was too grand a dream. I was a realist. What I sensed intuitively I wouldn't admit to myself consciously. How could I have a fine and eligible beau like James Burtin and not consider a future with him?

A girl with a handicap like mine should snatch any good man who came her way, right? I asked myself that question frequently and never settled on a satisfactory answer. The obvious answer didn't set well in my heart. Perhaps I had a crippled twisted heart too.

IN 1926 TRANSPORTATION could have been a problem for me. We'd seen many cars in magazines and newspapers and in Holden and Worcester. A simple vehicle could be purchased for $300. Papa made only $900 in a good year. I doubted he would want to own a car. He was comfortable with his animal-powered transportation, and they provided fertilizer for everything from Mama's special rose bushes to our large vegetable garden.

As I continued my secretarial training, I didn't want Papa to drive me into Worcester on the days he didn't have to go there. Axel drove me to 122A to catch a trolley into Worcester. Ebba often said I was hard on Axel, but I didn't think so. He seemed more like a ten-year-old than a six-year-old. I forgot how young he was and took advantage of his kindness and quickness. He'd gather his school things, harness the horse, and drive me to the trolley stop.

I didn't see that taking me to 122A was an extra effort for such a young boy. I took it for granted Axel liked helping me get to the trolley before he went to school. I felt independent on the trolley. Once aboard, it was an easy ride into Worcester. The trolley stopped at the corner of the Fairchild School's entrance.

Graduation would be in the first week of May. I presented a good appearance in each of my half dozen business outfits. Ebba and Mama helped me fit my clothes from the latest Butterick patterns. Mama sewed so fine anyone thought I wore store-bought clothes.

Representatives from companies visited the school at least once a week near graduation. They interviewed employment candidates. Mr. and Mrs. Fairchild were thoughtful in helping me present the best image to the interviewers. The interviews were arranged with me standing in front of the chair in which I would sit as the interview began.

When a company representative entered the room, I shook hands and then sat when the representative sat. I didn't have to walk in front of them. We chatted. I answered business-related questions.

My future employment was a regular concern in our family prayer time. Ebba told me my job was on the top of Mama's prayer list. We knew God knew our thoughts, and He was not forgetful. Mama also believed He wanted us to talk to Him about the desires of our hearts.

I didn't mind being the subject of conversation, hopes, and prayers. Mama told me fair pay, a caring employer, benefits, good co-workers, and my own strength and ability to continue learning and doing good work were in her prayers. I told her about them one afternoon while I snapped beans. The sit-down jobs were always mine.

"I am praying God will give you the best place, Annelise," she said. "It might not seem like the best job at first, but it will over time. He will place you where you will learn and thrive. We have to trust Him and leave it up to Him. You keep learning and applying, and something will come along. I'm sure of it."

She stopped to look me in the eye. "Always trust God to

lead you. This country has changed since I came. People are more independent from each other and from God. It doesn't feel right. When I look in God's Word, I read constant reminders that we are to trust and rely on Him. Don't be fooled by the worldly messages, Annelise. You're a smart pretty girl. I pray that you will see the way God has for you."

I kept snapping beans and tried not to betray my amazement at Mama's long talk. She never talked so much at once. I feel chagrined I took her love and prayers for granted. I resolved to pray more about my future and listen more to every person who interviewed Fairchild graduates.

Company representatives came from near and far. They interviewed for key secretarial positions, ones that led to an executive secretary. James now met me for lunch once a week. He was interested in my interviews.

I wondered if he ever thought about changing jobs. When I asked him, he said, "No. I'm doing fine. I'll be with the company for years. I like selling cars."

On the trolley ride home, I wondered how I felt about his contentment to stay in a pattern. I wanted to break patterns. I'd looked at apartments near downtown. I had read advertisements for rooms for rent, for boarding houses and boarder situations. One had a room and took meals with a family, which was less than apartment rent.

If I was offered a job in Worcester, I wanted to live there as an independent career woman. However, could I move away if Mama and Papa wanted me to stay? Would Ebba and Axel be shocked at my moving out? Did I owe my family compliance because they had raised me through infantile paralysis? Could I declare I would live my own life and still be a good Christian daughter and sister?

My family deserved more of my attention. I evaluated my desires about the future. I needed to talk with them, play the piano for Papa and games with Axel. Our family helped each other, but I knew my help and interactions were uneven.

I'd listened to girls at Fairchild Office School. Many had unhappy homes with parents who battled alcoholism or were cruel. The girls worked to escape their terrible situations. I never heard any of them mention church attendance or kind loving actions from their family members.

Little Axel did his chores in the morning and helped me. He kept up on his farm and household responsibilities like milking our cow and filling the wood box. He was a good student and with friends fished, hiked, and rode bikes with whenever they could gather.

Axel would become a special man, I sensed. He could do anything he set his mind to do. Mama and Papa had him as a special joy late in their life, so they were strict with him.

Ebba seemed the most vivacious member of our family. Interest in helping other people directed her choices. She was organized, and her best subject was math. She was as interested in the world, but preferred her life in Holden isolated from the world of cities.

People seemed more pleasant along the main street of Holden in the spring days. The winter crust of ice and gray snow melted, and the brisk air gave people hope. People talked of future plans for gardens and families. They spoke thankfully of having come through winter.

Ebba loved uplifting stories, and she didn't often hear them from me. She enjoyed news without gossip or negative judgments. If I was shocked at something someone said or did, I tried not to show it, but I'd discuss it with Ebba in the evening.

I played Mama's and Papa's favorite hymns on the piano in the evenings. They loved piano music and listened to me play for hours. Mama listened while she sewed or knit.

Sometimes she did tatting which created beautiful lace. She sold this in special fabric stores.

Papa read or meditated or prayed while listening to the piano. Sometimes he asked me to play another song just as the last notes of a song faded. Papa's relationship with God, his study of the Bible, his straightforward, hard-working life, his love for Mama and us, and his love of music made his core.

Sometimes he and Mama sat and held hands while I played their requests. Ebba and I had noticed that as our parents became older, they showed more affection in front of us. I wished James would show more interest in affection.

I did suggest buying a radio. James had one and said the programs were wonderful to hear in the evening. Papa said perhaps we would buy one, but did not seem motivated to shop for a radio. I thought I would end up buying one as a gift for the family.

In the evening Axel waited for me to descend from the trolley. He liked to drive the little cart because it went fast. He told me about the cars he'd own someday. He also told me that he would learn to fly a plane. His dreams made mine seem tame!

FINALLY AT THE start of summer of 1926, I took my first job at a new machine parts plant. It wasn't secretarial. Mainly I completed mailings, addressed envelopes, folded papers, and stuffed envelopes. I hoped the manager would move me to something else, but he didn't. The company was not run any better than it was in effectively using its workers' abilities.

I observed many problems in procedures and billing that led me to doubt they would stay in business. I shared my concerns with Ebba. She thought I had absorbed too much of Papa's negative ideas about the financial state of the nation. Although the nation seemed to be doing well, Papa persisted in saying we ought to save more against future tough times.

In January of 1927, the company officers announced we should find other jobs. They would close. They were sorry, but new businesses faced too many financial challenges.

Looking out the trolley's window that last work day, I cried. Now what? I doubted the Fairchild School would help me search for another employer. What business hired in the frozen month of January?

I dreaded Papa's typical evening questions. "What interesting happened in your day? How did the Lord guide you today? Is there something new to be thankful for? What did you learn? Who did you help today?" He'd asked these questions since we were in grade school.

Axel was thankful for scoring well on a science exam. Ebba's course work for an accounting certificate would be completed soon, and I said I was thankful I had a loving family to support me now that I was unemployed. Everyone stopped eating. They stared at me, and then looked at one another, then at me.

"The business has failed?" Papa asked.

"Yes. I didn't fail. The business did. Everyone who worked there is out of work. The owners packed their personal items, but everything else the bank will confiscate."

"Why wasn't there enough work for them, Papa?" Axel asked.

"Maybe there was enough work, son, but they didn't manage their business well. Annelise has explained before they didn't organize orders and projects well."

The rest of the dinner time remained quiet. Everyone was lost in his or her thoughts. I was thankful no one asked what

I would do now. I had no answer then but determined to find a new job within a month or two at the most.

In two weeks, I had employment as a general office worker. Through Papa, a company, for which he did mechanical repair work, hired me. They liked him so they hired his daughter in their growing office work.

Eyebrows raised when people saw I walked with a terrible limp. I held my head high and always tried to look fashionable. Mama was one of the best seamstresses, and Ebba and I created stylish hairdos on one another.

Ebba had a lovely high school graduation, and I received permission to take the afternoon off so I could attend the graduation ceremony. Ebba looked like an angel peeking out of a cloud in the special white batiste dress with a layer of white chiffon. Ebba was in the top five students and a member of the ProMerito Society for those who had earned high grades in all subjects all four years. Mama, Papa, Axel and I looked on proudly.

Hanne and Ingelise had sent graduation cards with five dollars in them. Ingelise also had a long encouraging note, advising Ebba to attend college. She wanted Ebba to get a four-year degree for a promising future of many career choices.

After the speeches, music, reception, and chats with neighbors, we headed home in the family wagon. Though cars were at the graduation, wagons and buggies outnumbered them. James waited at the house. He couldn't leave work to attend the graduation. He seemed like a member of our family. He had made trips to our house for three years.

That late June afternoon the parlor was open. Mama had decorated the room with fresh scented flowers. We drank her homemade fruit punch and watched Ebba open her cards and gifts. Axel gave Ebba tortoise shell hair combs. My gift was a silk scarf that brought out the blue of her eyes. Mama and Papa gave her a beautiful silver, feminine watch that pinned to a pocket or collar. James's gift was tan leather purse.

Ebba cried from happiness. I couldn't remember many times I was moved to tears of happiness. Most of my tears came from anger, frustration, or embarrassment. Ebba wiped her tears gracefully from her eyes.

As I watched James talk softly to Ebba, a chill chased down my spine while a pain zapped my heart. My fingers trembled. My stomach clenched into a knot. They looked good together. What a fine couple, heads together, discussing the watch and its engraved words: *Love from Mama and Papa.*

Our family budget had been much tighter when I graduated. I had a lovely silver chain necklace from Mama and Papa for my graduation. Had I ooooohed and aaahhhhed over it as Ebba did over the watch? Had I listened to advice from anyone like Ingelise? Had anyone given me advice? I could not remember.

When I had graduated, I had my mind on learning skills for my career. My plans must have been so obvious that no one offered advice. My inner need forced me to be strong and confident. I also worried I would travel life alone.

As I watched James and Ebba, the thought that I would forever be single came to me, but that would be better than marrying out of desperation. If James was not meant for me, but looked at Ebba the way I saw him looking at her, then he was meant for her. I felt my intuition had told me this a year ago, but I smothered the idea.

How could I tell James? Did he know? Did he have a clue that Ebba's sweetness had captured his heart far more firmly than my facts and quips?

Ebba surely didn't know, but she had been captivated by

James since he had first showed up at our door. The thought of Ebba and James belonging together appeared clear now to me. Had anyone else in the family noticed the way Ebba and James looked at one another? The dying embers of a dream of love and marriage blurred my eyes. I took a slow deep breath, held back tears and self-pity. An inner coldness worse than a frigid winter evening froze my heart.

13

CREDIT, CONFESSIONS, AND DISASTER

"Those who choose to have doves and be guardians of them must provide protection for them from the environment and predators." **Kind Planet Humane Education on Dove Care**

Ebba did not take Ingelise's advice. She entered a one-year accounting and business course in the fall 1927. When she graduated in August of 1928, a job waited for her.

I was still employed at the mechanical parts company, yet always looking for something better. I didn't voice my complaints to Mama and Papa. They found good in every situation. They wanted us to develop positive outlooks and thankful hearts. Many days I smiled on the outside giving no clue of my serrated heart.

Although I was not happy, the New York Yankee fans were happy that fall. The team beat the St. Louis Cardinals in the World Series. The Summer Olympic Committee Chairman, General Douglas MacArthur, were happy. Before the Olympics started, he had said, "We are here to represent the greatest country on Earth. We did not come here to lose gracefully. We came here to win–and win decisively."

The Americans won many medals. Those who thought women were mistreated in public competitions like the Olympics, were happier. Women were allowed to participate in track and field events. Pope Pius the IX disapproved and tried to sway the final opinion, but his opinion made no difference. Apparently, the Olympic Committee did not set their guidelines according to papal ideas or influence.

I wondered if Ingelise and Anthony discussed the papal pronouncement. I wondered how the Catholic believers could be certain the Pope was infallible. If they believed he was infallible, they'd have to believe women shouldn't compete in public sports events. That idea to me was ridiculous. I did gain some happiness from the fact that the Olympic Committee had not been swayed away from letting women compete in track and field events.

The Germans were happy. These games marked Germany's return to the Olympics after serving a ten-year probation for its *aggressiveness* in World War I. I wasn't sure what to think about the Germans rejoining the Olympics. When one looked at Germany's history, one could believe the Germans were not through causing trouble.

The Republicans were happy. Herbert Hoover was elected president in November, following Calvin Coolidge, so Republican power continued. Hoover sounded like an interesting man for the next President. He was the son of a Midwestern Quaker. He and his young wife had lived in China with his corporate job. The Boxer Rebellion broke out while Hoover and his wife were there. For a month they had lived in a settlement of foreigners under daily heavy fire in Tientsin. Mrs. Hoover worked in a hospital, and Hoover directed the barricading of buildings. Stories told of his rescuing people, including Chinese children.

Stock market investors were happy. Great technological advancements and wider markets were predicted. My Worcester employer didn't notice ups or downs. He plodded forward. I felt I was treading water. I longed to have a career with interesting work, good pay, benefits, fine co-workers, a wonderful boss. I had no money for the stock market, but I still had dreams.

The United States Federal Reserve was happy. They planned to stabilize the economy by raising the interest rates to discourage stock speculation. Most believed the government knew about such matters, and everyone saw our country was expanding through new inventions and technological developments. Wages had increased in the past few years, and people were happy about that. People were spending, buying items of their dreams, if not with cash, on credit. Buying on credit was becoming quite standard.

Papa and Mama considered buying on credit wrong. They bought what they could pay for and saved for what they could not afford. The only time Papa had swerved from this belief was to buy the farm and adjoining land. This weighed heavily upon him. Each year he paid off more of the principal and the interest.

No one we knew now had money to purchase property outright. Prices seemed much higher than when Papa had purchased our acres. Everyone expected people to buy on a mortgage and pay it over time. If I hadn't gotten sick as a toddler, Papa and Mama would have had more money saved sooner and mortgaged less to attain their home and farm. They had gone a long time paying off their bank debt.

My friends bought items on credit, things from clothing to cars. James encouraged people to buy cars on credit. His sales commissions were great. He always drove a new vehicle, but he didn't buy them. He drove them to advertise for his employer. James said our country was thriving financially and cities growing because of how manufacturing was growing.

When we talked about the nation's health and wondered when we'd find better jobs, Papa said the farmers didn't share the nation's growing wealth. Farmers barely held their own ability to provide for their families and to keep farming. James had no response for Papa's observations about farmers.

Ebba liked simple bookkeeping for a small company. Her job sounded boring to me, but she earned her own money, had a career, and had seen more of James than I did. I didn't mind, but she was confused and guilty. Every time I was alone with either of them, I tried to start the difficult conversation I knew should happen, but I never did.

That December we had little snow, but the weather was colder than ice. Several people on Bailey Road were frostbitten badly. Doctors couldn't repair the damage. They had fingers amputated and other skin patches on their faces removed. Folks predicted with cold and no snow, we'd have a summer drought.

The cold weather didn't end. Most years a thaw arrived in January or February, but not in 1929. When President Hoover was inaugurated on March 4th, it was too cold to celebrate.

After his inauguration, President Hoover promised a great four years ahead for our nation. At nineteen, I believed him. With my limited job and world experience, I thought Presidents knew what they talked about.

Our economy collapsing seemed far-fetched. In late March, businessmen in Worcester discussed new theories concerning possible bad times ahead for our economy. In less than a month with Hoover as President, people said his Presidency could be a miserable time for our nation. The only misery I saw was in the weather.

A traveling rag picker, named Haime, showed up regularly on Bailey Road. Haime did his route in all weather. People in Holden called him Haime the Jew. They said it as if it was a hyphenated name, Haime-the-Jew. It sounded mean to me, but I must confess I said it sometimes when I saw him.

Haime walked slowly beside his old horse and cart full of jumbled junk. He was tough and seemed to walk under layers of clothing from hats to boots. It was impossible to guess how many layers he wore over any part of his body. I wondered how he passed along Bailey Road every week and never suffered a tinge of frostbite.

Axel was the only person who enjoyed long conversations with Haime. I never heard Axel make a disparaging remark about Haime, and Axel never said Haime-the-Jew. What Axel could find to talk about with Haime baffled me, but Haime never passed by without Axel giving him some rags or bits of metal and having a conversation.

On a warm May evening of 1929, James and I stood in the front yard on our way to James's parked car. I could not avoid the conversation I had long dreaded, yet I felt he must have been waiting for this talk and had not had the courage to start it. I had one kind of conversation planned that I must have with James and a different sort with Ebba.

I had noticed that Ebba blushed when she looked directly at James, and he looked confused when he spent time with the family. His ease with me had disappeared sometime over the past months. This May night I knew I must speak to him and I had to sound positive.

"James, before you leave, I want to say something I should have long ago."

"What's that Annelise?"

"I don't think of you any longer as my beau. You're like my family. Being at our home is a comfortable habit for you, and my family thinks of you as a part of our family. I want to be clear, James. I don't foresee marrying you. I like you only as a friend."

"But Annelise—"

"Let me finish James. Whatever love my parents have between them, we don't have it. There's a connection there that goes from looks they exchange to the soul. Their love is like a tangible connection. If I ever marry, that's what I want."

"Why? Annelise, I—"

"I'm not finished. You have to analyze your own feelings, James. I've observed you many evenings here in our home, and you enjoy time with Ebba. James, you matter to her. She is used to having you come to visit and her attention is focused on you when you are here with the family. You may have started visiting here because of me, but I think your affection has changed focus."

"What? What are you saying, Annelise?"

He sounded stunned, really shocked—but I didn't know if it was over what I had to say about us, or over what I was revealing about him and Ebba.

"Ebba is beautiful and sweet, James. She is smart and capable. Truthfully, she cares about you, I guess she even loves you. Ebba would be a good wife."

"Annelise! You're throwing me over and recommending your sister to me as a potential wife?"

"I'm not wrong. Don't act so shocked. Think about it. She

draws your attention. You give her special gifts, attention, gentle looks. She is the one you should be courting."

"She's so . . . so young. She . . ."

"She'll age, James. Keep visiting, but switch your attention to Ebba. Talk with my parents about it if you want. Talk with her. I don't mind. My family will accept it, too. When I consider my future, marriage isn't in the picture."

"Annelise, that's odd for a woman to say. I thought *all* women dreamed of marriage." James had a tone mixing embarrassment with exasperation.

"That's not accurate, James. Society *expects* women to marry. Not all women desire it. Look at the famous women, the women who have changed this country."

"Famous women who have changed the country?"

"I'm not surprised they don't come to your mind. I doubt I could find a man who could name ten of those women."

"But I'm sure you can." He sounded aggravated. His masculine air of superiority annoyed me. I took a deep breath and tried to drown him in names.

"Yes, James, I can: Virginia Dare, Emma Willard, Lucy Stone, Sarah Grimke, Lucretia Mott, Mary Lyon, Elizabeth Cady Stanton, Harriet Tubman, Amelia Jenks Bloomer, Sojourner Truth, Harriet Beecher Stowe, Abbey Kelley Foster, Susan B. Anthony, Julia Ward Howe, Victoria Woodhull, Virginia Louisa Minor, Belva Lockwood, Alice Stone Blackwell, Jeanette Rankin, Edith Wharton, Anna Howard Shaw, Ida B. Wells, Mary Dreier, Alice Paul, Rebecca Felton, Gertrude Ederle . . ."

"Stop! You're overwhelming me in more ways than you realize. I am sure you are right about their being independent-minded with higher goals than marriage. You amaze me, Annelise, with all you have stored inside your brain. Your quick intelligence is part of what attracted me to you.

Our luncheon conversations, our competition over who knew the most unusual facts about Worcester presented a challenge.

"You can hide it well, but you like to win, Annelise. Sometimes you *need* to win. You're small, petite, feminine, stylish, but strong, iron-willed, bright-eyed, and brilliant, not shy, but you're not loud and rude like other modern girls. You seemed like you might depend on a man you loved."

"I'm modern, but I might still consider a marriage someday."

"You are not completely modern. And you know it. Modern girls these days frequently smoke and drink. They are more lax in their standards with the opposite sex. We've kept company for years and only exchanged a few kisses."

"You only–"

"Never mind. You didn't fall in love with me, Annelise, and I must have sensed that. So, I didn't fall in love with you. I love being with you and your family. I feel like I've known them all my life, and I want to continue to know them. I have little family left, just cousins. You have a wonderful family, more wonderful than you realize."

"And Ebba–"

"She is special and touches my heart in a way that–"

"In what way?"

"All right. Ebba touches my heart in a way you haven't."

"I knew it."

"I don't mean that badly, Annelise."

"I don't take it badly. We have to be honest, James. Ebba would be better wife for you. If we are true friends, and perhaps in-laws one day, we should be honest with each other. I am hoping this conversation won't drive you away from us all. I am hoping we can still be friends, but that's all. You should look to Ebba. Once she realizes you and I are only friends, she will let her feelings about you blossom."

"You are comfortable acting as a matchmaker for your sister?"

"I am. You are slow in courtship and she has certainly held a rein on her emotions concerning you because she thought of you as my beau. That has changed now. You can improve in your second attempt at courtship with someone else in this family who is sweeter, kinder, and more feminine in traditional ways than I am."

James laughed, but not with happiness. Suddenly, near Mama's roses, he hugged me hard and fast. I felt great strength with his arms around me and the rush of worry that I had made the wrong decision. He was strong, smelled clean as the woods, and his chest was so solid against my face. My body was pulled tight to his, fiercely for a moment. Then he released me. It had been a passionate hug of saying goodbye to someone dear. I had made him understand I was serious. There would be no future of any romantic kind for him and me.

James had never pulled me to him in such a strong way before that evening. I sensed relief in that hug. James had been honest when he said he had not fallen in love with me. I felt off-balance and stepped back away from him with a stagger. He laughed again, a short cursory sound, said goodnight, and drove away.

I lingered outside. Had I made a mistake? I wanted to be loved. I wanted to experience passion and romance. I wanted the thrill of being desired by an admirable man. I wanted a man strong physically, mentally, and emotionally. I think I wavered on James in the emotional aspect, but then we had been closed off to one another emotionally. How fair could I be in my estimation?

Examining my heart and I knew the truth of my feelings for James. He was no more for me than I was for him in marriage. Yet in his arms I had felt the possibility of passion. What if I had been a modern girl and encouraged his physical proximity and welcomed his advances much earlier? Maybe love would have sparked between us. Maybe I would have felt a passion that led me to decide James was right for me.

I stood in the cool evening and thought and thought. More sighs escaped me than I could count. My limp seemed more pronounced as my body felt heavy, awkward, and sad. Still, when I returned to the house, I was still sure I had made the right decision.

Later, as Ebba and I lay beside one another in our bed, I told her. "Ebba, tonight I told James I'm not in love with him."

She gasped and turned toward me, propped on her elbow. "**Why** did you say that? Is he heartbroken? Is he coming back? Oh, Annelise, how could you say such things to him?"

"Because I know he likes someone better than me, someone he can love and marry. He is not heartbroken because at the end of our conversation he laughed and hugged me. He felt free. I am sure of it."

"Free? Of you? Of us all?" Fear and anger filled her eyes, my dear Ebba was furious with me.

"Oh, no, Ebba, not us all. He feels free because he knows how I feel, and he faced his feelings. He's smart enough to sort things out right."

I heard her sigh deeply with the catch of a sob. She flopped on the bed, so I turned toward her and kept talking. "Ebba, I am sure he will be back. He told me he loved being with our family."

"Oh," was all Ebba said as a mixture of a cry and a sigh.

She shivered, sighed again and said softly, "You said James faced that he cares about someone else. He admitted that? That he loves someone else?"

Ebba's disappointment was clear. I would change that. How surprised she would be!

"He is more attracted to her than to me. He likes her enough for it to be love. I think it probably is love, but he has to wait and see how she feels. She's younger than I am and has just been relating to James as a friend."

"Then I doubt he will be coming here very much. He will want to have more time to be with her. Do you know her?" Ebba's voice was a soft whisper.

"Of course, I do, you silly goose."

"You really do? Annelise, how could you not tell me? How long have you suspected James might be in love with her?"

"I do know her, and I probably knew long ago that James cared for her, but I wouldn't admit it to myself. Then I couldn't very well say anything to you about it could I?"

"Who is she Annelise?"

"Ebba, she is *you*."

"What?"

She sat up straight. In the moonlight with her hands on her crossed knees, she looked alive and electrified. "What do you mean?"

"Ebba, James has found it difficult not to just focus on you during his visits here for months, maybe a year. I told him he'd better face facts because marriage has to be based on real heart-to-heart connections. I told him to see if you feel the same way. I thought you cared for him more than a friend."

"You didn't? Oh Annelise, I can't believe you! I don't! How dare you match-make for me? It's embarrassing, Annelise! It's horrifying!"

"Don't be ridiculous, Ebba. You are thrilled. How can you say you don't have feelings for him? You little liar! You are lying to yourself as much to me! You blush deep rosy red when he gives you attention or a compliment. Your eyes almost water when you stare at him, and you always ask about him. I am matchmaking because I care about you both. I want happiness for you! If you find it with James, that's fine. I'd like to have both of you in my life, happily married to each other."

～

JAMES SEEMED EVEN SLOWER at courting Ebba. I guessed my words had set him to the hard work of sorting his feelings. He rarely visited during the summer. When he appeared, Ebba perked up. When he went a few days between visits, Ebba acted unlike her normally cheerful self. I was miserable watching her hopes and emotions rise and fall.

I informed Mama and Papa about ending my romantic ideas about James. They covered any startled reaction. I know they prayed for James and Ebba that summer because James did not stop by often. Ebba lost much of her sparkle and smiles. Some people believed the adage of girls being made of sugar and spice and everything nice. Therefore, parents of daughters should have a smooth road.

Anyone who talked to Mama and Papa would have new insight into raising boys and girls. If one looked from Inge-lise's conversion to Catholicism, to Hanne's hot-and-cold affection, to a crippled daughter who could not be satisfied with all that was good, to another daughter on the verge of heartbreak no sugar appeared and the spice might be jalapeno. Axel, the boy, seemed the only child in our family who might be easy to raise.

Our family was busy with crops, canning, preserving, drying, and caring for the animals. We had all had jobs and responsibilities as long as we could remember. Ebba and I had our own income that we tithed, as Mama and Papa had taught us.

We saved too. Ebba was better at saving than I was, but we did agree on some uses of money, like choosing to give Mama and Papa money toward household expenses. We hoped to help pay for ordinary items. Then Papa and Mama could use their extra money to pay off the farm mortgage.

Axel played with his friends, always had his chores done, made inventions out of junk Haime sold or gave to him, read newspapers, and helped Papa with our dairy customers and Mama by selling jams, jellies, and fresh fruit in town. Axel was the busiest boy we knew, and seemed so much more mature than other boys his age. He also retained his kind heart and respectful nature. Anyone who ever watched him having an animated conversation with Haime would see Axel had sincere respect for the man.

Our farm continued to thrive as Papa had planned and planted with an eye for growth and respect for the land. Our farm included huge raspberry bushes, great stands of blackberries, a quarter of an acre of strawberries, select patches of wild blueberries that Papa tended and cultivated, and peach, pear, and apple trees. Between Mama's flowers, the vegetables, and the fruits, bees found our acres a bit of heaven.

Papa's and Mama's dream was coming to fruition. In the twilight of a September evening, the orange and yellow on the upper leaves, the cows lowing, fading chatter from the chicken coop, Axel zooming around the yard on his bicycle created a sense of fulfillment.

Mama knitting in her favorite rocker, Ebba and Papa reading, and me, playing the piano, life was good. I didn't have the job I had hoped for and was still at home, but life was whole and renewing on our farm. I could look around in an evening and see much to inspire thanksgiving.

Sometimes I thought Mama and Papa looked their ages and sometimes they seemed far younger than their years, like when they sat near one another and held hands, or took a walk in the twilight. Ebba loved to see them happy and together. I felt concern as her expression revealed she worried about love in her own life, love that would lead to marriage.

In late September 1929, I heard the downtown business owners talk only about a Bear market. I knew that meant the stock market and investments were bad.

One September day I purchased a motion picture magazine for twenty-five cents to read on the trolley home. Fay Wray was on the cover, looking gorgeous. Why do certain items and days stand out clearly?

Mama met me at the trolley stop. She had been out with the pony cart taking homemade goodies to elderly folks. It was a treat to have a late afternoon ride with Mama.

At the house, James was in the yard. He was playing catch with Axel. Ebba sat on an Adirondack chair on the porch. Papa had made two such chairs. She looked happy watching Axel and James playing catch.

"Hello!" I called to James and Axel as I carried a few packages toward the house.

Mama left the carriage for Axel to unhitch the horse and put away. James relieved me of the largest package. He did the same for Mama, and then he slowed to walk next to me.

"Annelise, I want you to know I've made investments that will move me forward in courting Ebba," he said softly with a shy smile.

"Why, James, I hear the market is risky. Ebba is not a girl

looking for a rich man. She wants a good man who will be a partner in a life together like Papa with Mama."

"I don't know if anyone can match your parents, Annelise." James had a tone of sadness as he walked away from me. He went off with Axel to see something in the barn, an invention of Axel's. When they emerged from the barn, Axel had James laughing so hard tears appeared in his eyes. Axel accomplished this when he recounted his experiences selling berries. Axel hardly had the proper methods for successful sales.

I said, "Good day, Mrs. Vandervort. I don't suppose you want any of these old berries," that's what Axel claimed he said at the start of his attempt to sell berries. As a career salesman, James was amazed Axel managed to sell any berries with such a negative opening, but then James said our berries looked so delicious that they sold themselves. Axel asked him questions about how to start a talk about selling something. For an hour James and Axel practiced various sales talk techniques.

The remaining hours of the evening were very relaxed. It was late when James left us. I think after a full day and lots of fresh air, we all fell asleep quickly that night.

The next day everything changed.

I was to meet Ebba in Worcester to shop. She had to buy two birthday presents for friends and wanted to find something for Elenora, Ingelise's only child. Poor Ingelise. She had probably thought she would give that handsome Italian a whole flock of children, but she didn't. We never knew the reason.

I met Ebba on the corner of Park and Dover Street. We joked about the weather clouding. After we shopped in two stores, a steady drizzle began. We walked uphill to Highland, a tough task for me. My ability to walk far and fast never matched my desire to do so. People were leaving work and crowded the sidewalk.

We took the trolley back to Holden. There were few stretches of any sidewalk in Holden, but now the sidewalk was so crowded that Ebba and I and a few others stepped into the street. Holden had a respectable number of cars, but people must have been waiting for the rain to lessen.

For a few minutes, there seemed little car, cart, or wagon traffic. Ebba walked next to the street and I walked next to the sidewalk's curb. We walked and talked in the drizzle and laughed a bit over people who feared getting even a little bit wet.

The motor and tail pipe on an old wreck of a truck created a lot of noise behind us. Lots of people were looking in that direction. I turned to check the vehicle's position when it careened toward us. Instinctively I pulled back, yanking at Ebba, but I was too slow.

Not only crippled by polio, but hit by a truck! That thought ran through my mind as I fell. I wondered if I would be crippled worse. I felt sharp pain from my arm as I heard Ebba's scream. Quiet Ebba, who hardly spoke loud enough to be heard screamed! I had heard a crack in my left arm as I fell and tumbled down the street. People shouted and ran. A couple people rushed to help me.

"Where is my sister?" I tried to push myself into a sitting position and asked the question over and over.

People who were helping me up looked at the street. Ebba laid face-down in the other direction! She moaned and whimpered. The truck's old bumper had hooked her skirt, maybe her leg, and dragged her down the street until someone rushed to stop the drunken driver.

My heart nearly stopped at the idea of sweet, graceful Ebba as a cripple. I couldn't even think past that to anything like injuries that would cause death. Blood covered her clothes. People surrounding her gasped. Two men knelt on the road, one on each side of her. I felt faint, but people supported me and helped me toward her. Ebba was hurt severely, and it had happened in a minute.

Axel was to meet us at a set time. Young and responsible, he had waited at the meeting point which was just a block away. He noticed a group standing on the curb up the street. A police officer had joined that group.

After securing the wagon, since he didn't see us, Axel walked toward the crowd. Then Axel noticed me in the backseat of the police car. I felt fear and pain. Ebba had just been taken to the hospital. The police officer would take me there too.

Axel leaned to the car window fear filled his eyes. "Annelise! What happened? Where's Ebba?"

14

GUILT, PROSPECTS, PROPOSAL, AND PERSEVERANCE

"There is an unacceptably high wounding rate in dove hunting. Studies indicate a wounding rate that exceeds twenty percent in hunted areas, which means one in five doves is wounded and not retrieved after being shot." **Humane Society of the United States**

Axel took a weight of guilt on himself. He had been late to meet us. He thought if he had come along earlier, he might have driven the buggy farther down the street and found us before the truck crashed into us. I could not convince him that even if he had been on time, the accident would have happened. We affirmed his innocence often.

Over time, he understood and freed himself from the false guilt. I on the other hand, the older sister, had let Ebba walk on the more dangerous street side while I had walked next to the curb. I knew Ebba was always protective of me, but I should have acted more like an older sister and been the one to walk on the street side. No one could convince me otherwise. The guilt I felt I would live with for the rest of my life.

While Ebba stayed a month in the Holden hospital, the world fell apart. My company, after the stock market crash, laid me off and many others. The company Ebba worked for went out of business by November. One positive out of the mess came with the news all Ebba's medical expenses were paid by the truck company.

People at all work levels across our nation had ignored the problem signs in the stock market. Extremely rich people became poor in one day. Papa had nothing invested in the stock market, but banks holding his savings folded. Fear and panic ran rampant through the nation.

Ebba was tucked away in painful misery in the hospital in Holden. At least she was unaware of the financial losses of her family, friends, and nation for a few weeks. There were rare days she had any relief from pain. Even with medication she felt pain and no one wanted to add to her misery by sharing the bad news that followed the stock market crash.

James was the only salesman his employer kept. James had worked the longest and sold the most cars for Bland Motors. James felt nervous but believed people would eventually buy cars as the nation rose out of the slump. Transportation moved toward all mechanical vehicles, according to James. Axel agreed with James and had many questions for him.

Papa said, "I mean no offense to your career choice James, but I'll never buy a car."

Mama considered the stock market crash a reckoning for our country that had embraced the wild aspects of the roaring 20s. Maybe she was right. Prosperity had been uneven and lavish lifestyles glorified. With extremely poor, needy and homeless people, it seemed outrageous some people to live like royalty, like the country had no economic worries

The stock market crash affected other countries. As I sat with my left arm in a restrictive cast and watched fall sunsets from the porch, James tried to explain the monetary mess to Axel and me. The overuses of credit, speculating on stock, the corrective measures for financial patterns caused the market to plummet. James was patient, but I was still confused. Papa listened as he read the paper and made occasional comments.

Our evening devotionals found Papa frequently choosing readings on trusting in the Lord and living according to God's standards. We also tried to find something to be thankful for in each part of our day. Each of us prayed for Ebba's recovery as a part of the list of needs we took before God each day.

We visited Ebba regularly. Sometimes I stayed with her for a long afternoon visit while Mama did other errands in town. Shortly before Ebba was to come home, she smiled at me like she'd felt a fresh arrow from Cupid's bow. I stared intently, guessing the reason for her fabulous smile, but I wanted to hear it from her.

"Are you going to tell me why you have on such a silly smile?" I asked.

"Is it a silly smile, Annelise? I just feel happy. James left here about an hour ago. He has visited me a couple times every week. He said he had a long talk with Papa. James said that if I would be happy as a married lady, he'd like to be the man who marries me."

"What?"

"Do you really need me to say it again?"

"No, I just think . . . it is an odd proposal, Ebba. You have to admit that is not a normal proposal."

"It wasn't a formal proposal. I think he will ask me more appropriately when I am home. He just needed to have an idea of my feelings."

"Don't you want a more romantic proposal?"

"I am sure that will come. James didn't want to continue visiting our family if there was no hope of me marrying him. He said that would be like torture to see me and know there was no hope for me to be his wife. That's romantic, isn't it?"

"It truly is." I took her hand with my good one. "We're quite a pair, aren't we, Ebba? My broken arm and gimpy leg, and your broken leg and gimpy heart."

"Gimpy heart! The things you say, Annelise! Should I tell Mama and Papa about my talk with James?" she asked.

"I think you should wait until James says the formal, romantic proposal. If he has talked to them about the marriage, they will know it's coming. They knew you were in love with him, just as I did."

"Did they?"

"I think even Axel knew, and you know how little he cares to think about romance."

"I got a note today from Hanne. Mama and Papa will be happy. Hanne wants to return to look for a hospital job in our area. She said she never really settled in Pennsylvania, never felt like it was home."

"And you'll be happy to have her back?" I asked her.

"Of course. Won't you? She's our older sister."

"What has that meant other than an occasional card with $5? We hardly know her, Ebba."

"You sound hard-hearted, Annelise. You aren't really like that."

"I'll trust your evaluation of me for now. I'll not argue with someone still on a long recovery road."

"Thanks for that!"

Mama had visited other folks in the hospital and arrived with smiles and affection. Her smile broadened as Ebba told her about Hanne. Tears filled Mama's eyes as she said, "I will be so happy to tell your father." I thought I understood her tearful joy as a mixture of relief that one of their chicks was coming home to roost. I think we all believed Hanne would not venture far away again.

That evening, I thought about Hanne's return. I hoped I'd like Hanne when she was back in our lives. I wondered if her years of distance from the family would make her value us more. I wondered if any news she would tell us of Ingelise would make Mama and Papa sad. Now, I thought I understood why she had resented me and followed Ingelise, but I couldn't imagine I would ever feel close to Hanne. I hoped she would be a better sister in her return.

I was twenty-two. For years I had built a hedge around my wounds. Although I had not shared my special resource of inspiration with my family, it was Helen Keller's words that helped me keep my wounds and challenges in perspective. Even Anne Sullivan, who had lost most of her eyesight before joining the Keller household, was an inspiration to me. I thought often of these two women, who struggled much as I did and who overcame their disabilities.

I had no job prospects. Helen Keller said, "No pessimist ever discovered the secret of the stars or sailed to an uncharted land or opened a new heaven to the human spirit. "The love of my life intended to marry my younger sister. Helen Keller said, "Character cannot be developed in ease and quiet. Only through experiences of trial and suffering can the soul be strengthened, vision cleared, and success achieved."

An older sister, who had never shown me special affection, was coming home, to probably a great welcome. Helen

Keller's words, "Self-pity is our worst enemy, and if we yield to it, we can never do anything wise in this world."

I lived at home with a broken arm and crippled leg, dependent on my parents. Helen Keller reminded people, "Be of good cheer. Do not think of today's failures, but of the success that may come tomorrow. You have set yourselves a difficult task, but you will succeed if you persevere; and you will find joy in overcoming obstacles."

With Hanne's return, no job security, and Ebba's marriage to James, I would soon see how well I could take Helen's words to heart. Could the words I had memorized build strength against such personal challenges?

15

ELOPEMENT, DEPRESSION, RECOVERY

"I have a one-legged female dove, a homing bird, and she has a deformed leg. It grew so it turned almost backward. The vet broke that leg and turned it when the dove was just three weeks old. The vet put a cast on the leg and splinted it. We hoped she could use it after it healed, but these efforts were unsuccessful. Her leg still springs backward, toward her tail and won't stay where it is supposed to when she tries to stand or walk. I never cut the wings of this dove so that she can fly. Let's face it, if I did that, she couldn't move at all. She has learned to scoot when she has to move just a little, but most of the time she flies when she needs to get somewhere."
Dove Breeder in California

The furniture company with the wild truck driver compensated us financially for our pain and suffering. I didn't know how money could remunerate for our terror and pain, but I was glad to have the money. I received a third of Ebba's payment. I *only* had a broken arm, a quick healing break. Ebba's leg was badly broken. Her beautiful alabaster skin had been ripped, scraped, torn, and burned along one side of her body from foot to ribs.

She stayed a long time in the hospital and had weeks of recovery at home. Ebba's life was tranquil when she was young, and difficult after the accident. She was strong as Mama and Papa had taught us to be in body, soul, mind, and spirit.

Ebba and I had wanted a car. The settlement not only paid Ebba's bills, but paid for her to buy a new car and provided still more money she planned to save for married life.

James helped her choose a two-toned, white-and-blue Pontiac. For Ebba that might have been almost as exciting as marriage. The country in depression did not invite big celebrations. Their wedding was reserved, private, and uneventful. It took place months after Ebba purchased the Pontiac. I told Ebba I couldn't imagine a wedding that wasn't equal to a car purchase. That was my opinion. She just shook her head as if to shake away my tempting thoughts of a larger fancy wedding.

Axel went over the car's features with Ebba. Having a car at our house was a pinnacle event for a young man with an eye and mind for modern inventions. Axel was able to explain simple mechanical questions to Ebba. He had helped Papa with the farm machinery and bought junk pieces from Haime to fix machines Papa thought were hopeless. Axel would take something apart, put it together with other pieces, and that something worked.

James taught Ebba how to drive. At age ten, Axel asked to go along so he took driving lessons with Ebba. James was a good teacher. He gave clear directions and was never shocked or angry by a mistake.

Axel volunteered to care for the car. He sheltered the car

in a section of the barn and kept it clean and polished. He enjoyed this responsibility. I thought he probably imagined the day he would care for his own car.

Ebba planned to find another job before she drove regularly. To keep up her driving skills, she chauffeured Mama on her errands. Though Ebba kept a smile, I often thought she moved as if she was in pain. Ebba's leg healed slowly. She told me she had fallen out of the wheelchair when she was alone in the hospital. She had called for help. No staff person came.

Since the wheelchair's brake was on the wheelchair, she had pulled herself up by grabbing the wheelchair's brake. Eventually she scooted to the bed. Ebba wondered if she had broken another bone in that fall. She needed a reason for what seemed like very slow healing.

James had been attentive through Ebba's long recovery and formally proposed on May Day, 1930. However, they shared no wedding plans. Mama wanted to give Ebba at least a simple wedding. Ebba was the only daughter she could help with planning a wedding, but Mama was never one to force her own wishes. Mama just told Ebba that she would be glad to help with wedding plans in any way.

Hanne tried to make Ebba plan a wedding. She nagged Ebba, but Ebba showed a quiet strength against pressure from anyone about making plans or help with the wedding. Hanne relinquished hope about discussing the wedding. She was happily established with a job in the Worcester hospital, and Hanne was dating. Hanne revealed this information carefully, not knowing what Mama and Papa would think. Mama and Papa had nothing negative to say to Hanne about dating. We all treated Hanne more like a long-term friend than a daughter when she returned. Hanne and I did not mesh in temperament. We spoke politely with one another.

By July, Ebba had found a bookkeeper job for the Olson Company. That company had not taken good times for granted. Their good planning and savings carried them through the months after the stock market crash. Pleased, they were happy to employ Ebba.

Front Street of downtown Worcester, MA, mid 1920s.

When Ebba told her employer of her autumn wedding plans, she received congratulations and a promise that she could take time off to have an autumn honeymoon trip.

Ebba's employer also congratulated Papa on Ebba's wedding. Papa talked about it at dinner without realizing that no one else in the family had heard this news.

Can you imagine our surprise? That's how the family discovered James and Ebba planned to marry in the fall. Papa fell silent at the sight of the surprise on our faces.

Ebba explained, "James and I talked about marriage. The wedding will be small. I am uncomfortable with the extra expense when our country is financially miserable, so many people are unemployed and homeless."

Well, I thought, *leave it to Ebba to think of sacrifice at the time of her wedding.*

If I had planned my wedding then, I would have found a way to celebrate even with a conservative amount of money. I would not have pared down my wedding for the sake of appearances or to show sympathy for the country. Enough people felt the sadness of scarcity.

With very minimal wedding expenses, Ebba explained that she and James would buy furniture with her funds. They could afford to buy anything they might need to set up housekeeping. Ebba was business-like and organized. I knew James would go along with whatever his pretty young sweet life wanted.

A bigger shock came when Ebba and James left for a day trip to New Hampshire, and it turned out they had really gone away to elope. None of our family attended the ceremony, or had any opportunity to choose to attend the wedding. I couldn't believe Ebba had done that to Mama and Papa. How could Ebba, the darling youngest daughter, plan and enjoy a wedding without her family?

Didn't she consider Mama would have loved to sew her dress and help plan, and that Papa would have loved to escort her down the aisle? Axel would have been an outstanding usher and I, a bridesmaid? I was hurt and resentful and showed my anger to Ebba and James.

When I had my first conversation with Ebba, now Mrs. Burtin, I asked her if she was pregnant. Her face turned red as instantly as if I had slapped both her cheeks. I did not mean it sarcastically or meanly. Surely only something that drastic would have caused her to elope.

Ebba was horrified that I thought she might be pregnant. After the deep blush faded from her face, she looked pale. She was always innocent, sweet even after her worst trials. In my heart I knew Ebba would be a virgin until marriage.

Mama and Papa were slightly comforted when Ebba told

them the minister had been an old friend of our family. His wife had been their only witness. Ebba and James showed us the certificate and described the wedding, held in a parsonage room.

The minister's wife played the piano while Ebba and James took their vows, and then congratulated them as soon as her husband pronounced them married. On the way home, Ebba and James stopped at an inn for light supper before driving to Massachusetts.

James had the grace to look embarrassed about the elopement. He said Ebba had wanted it. She had campaigned for their own private wedding for weeks, and since he loved her, he wanted her wedding day to be just what she chose.

For years afterwards, when I thought of Ebba's elopement, a wave of anger ran through me, followed by a wave of sadness. I felt cheated and thought Ebba had cheated Mama and Papa as well.

Hanne looked surprised at first, then just serious. It seemed like she had figured something out about Ebba's elopement that the rest of us did not know. One day when I complained about Ebba's elopement, Hanne said quietly, "Maybe Ebba didn't want the person who had dated James for years at the wedding. Have you thought how she must wonder about his feelings and attention for you? I think Ebba was wise to opt for an elopement. It was totally her day with James. We should just be happy for her." I didn't say anything back to Hanne.

Until they found an apartment a month later, James lived in his small rented room and Ebba at home with us. I shook my head at their choices and wondered if they really loved one another in a depth fit for marriage. Did people in love act so dispassionately? How could they be in love, be married, and choose to live apart? I didn't want that kind of love. A great passion must capture my heart.

My doubts about Ebba and James, love, and so many choices muddled my mind. The New Testament book of James warned against being consumed by doubts. We as a family had read those verses about living in doubt wavering back and forth many times. I doubted Ebba would be happy in marriage. I doubted that Hanne's return was a good thing. I doubted I would have a career. Though I knew doubt wasn't wise, I continued doubting, thinking negatively, and a spirit of bitterness grew in me.

My search for wisdom that could erase my doubts started me looking in many places. I felt tossed like a leaf on the wind. I wanted an enduring love relationship, a solid love. I wanted to be so assured of love that I could travel to a distant country and know my love would protect and sustain me. I wanted a passion, protection, and commitment like that of the love Boaz had for Ruth.

My wavering ideas also saw marriage as a trap, a weight worse than my crippled leg, dependency and confinement, submission, and limits. I knew most marriages were not like my parents' marriage, and yet they had lived separated in the early years of their marriage while my father worked in America to earn money to send for my mother. The comfort they felt with one another, even tenderness, appeared when they were together.

James and Ebba appeared to be in love. Both were reserved. I resolved to pray more for them and about my attitude. My negative thoughts needed to be curtailed, but I would not surrender my hopes of a career and independence. These were difficult times, but I could continue to learn all I could in each temporary job. At least I regularly had calls to report for a temporary office job.

I worked at different office jobs short term, a month here, a week there, specialty jobs, filing reorganization, whole billing systems, and mailings. I gained experience to add to a resumé. I reminded myself to be grateful for any paying work, and Mama and Papa echoed that sentiment.

President Hoover was a millionaire. He embraced something called laissez-faire, which left everyone to find his own survival. Both Republicans and Democrats were upset with President Hoover. Our country and town struggled.

As January 1931 passed, Hanne shared an apartment with two nurses and kept company with a hospital staff member, George McCauley. He was an administrator for the hospital's food department. Though they both had Baptist upbringings, neither he nor Hanne attended church regularly.

Axel was interested in any sermons and loved church music. He had a good voice and planned to sing in the choir when he became a teenager. I chose to attend the Nazarene Church to feel more like an independent adult. Sometimes Axel visited with me.

We went to First Baptist in Holden with Mama and Papa when weather was bad. Some how we all maintained our faith even though times grew more difficult financially. No end was in sight to the country's dismal financial picture. People said if the country elected a different President that would help the nation.

By 1932, Holden suffered the same woes as the rest of the country. All the town employees had their wages cut by more than fifteen percent. The town had reduced or eliminated all they could to save money. Even lighting the streets in the morning was discontinued, no lights after 11p.m. More individuals applied for welfare. All the schools, except high school, had the telephones removed. Vocational classes were dropped at the high school. Eighth grade graduation was discontinued when Axel was in that grade.

With people earning so much less, unpaid taxes were serious for individuals and towns. Holden was one of the hardest hit towns by the Depression. Records showed 316 towns in the state, and Holden was 280thin collection of taxes. More money was paid out in welfare than the town had collected for taxes.

Papa and Mama continued to work the farm. Axel and I helped. My dreams hadn't been smothered but they seemed distant, like wishful thinking. I didn't think about marriage except to wonder why I didn't long for it. I did want romance. I wanted to feel attractive to young men, the way I had felt with James. No candidates were available.

In 1932 I voted the first time for a President. Our family didn't discuss personal decisions about the candidates and rarely discussed politics. I voted for Franklin Delano Roosevelt, a distant cousin of former President Theodore Roosevelt. Franklin Roosevelt had served as New York governor before he was sworn in as the thirty-second President of the United States in 1933.

Roosevelt's politics were much different from Teddy's. As I had wholeheartedly liked Teddy, I liked Franklin. It amazed me our President was usually in a wheelchair. He had been stricken with polio as a child, too. I knew this man in a way only polio survivors understood as they longed for people to see beyond their crippled feature.

Franklin Roosevelt's main goal focused on ending the Great Depression. His New Deal programs and policies provided work and immediate relief. His wife stood by his side at public ceremonies. I liked her demeanor. She wasn't a beauty, but had a great spirit.

President Roosevelt talked about long-term recovery and

reform. His ideas were to revive the economy. His optimism, strong speeches, and charm convinced us we had made the right decision in a President. His new phrases gave us quotes to use like the convincing motto: *nothing to fear but fear itself.*

The repeal of the 18thamendment—prohibition of alcoholic beverage sales—upset conservative and religious people. That prohibition amendment was repealed with the ratification of the 21stamendment. James drank a little, so did Hanne and George. Mama and Papa acknowledged that the apostle Paul had recommended people take a little wine for their stomachs. However, they did not choose to imbibe any alcoholic beverages.

Congress approved Roosevelt's ideas quickly. The programs didn't provide immediate relief of the oppressive poverty, but hope grew in the nation. The Civilian Conservation Corps employed thousands. Federal aid developed Worcester's airport. Concrete was poured at huge projects like the Hoover Dam. An emergency bank bill enabled banks to open and be solvent. Fireside chats became regular occurrences and soothed the nation's troubled spirit. Some mocked his speeches and the catchy phrases, but not my parents. They were respectful of our national leaders and prayed for them as much as they prayed for our family.

Congress worked extra hard. Newspapers called the time The Hundred Days, as if they were the most important days for our country. They passed many bills. The act my parents disliked most was the Beer Act, which raised the percentage of alcohol in a person's system before he or she was considered intoxicated.

President Roosevelt wanted to relieve people from all kinds of oppression, even having liquor illegal and restricted. I understood that point of view. But I did not voice my thoughts at home. Papa and Mama felt discouraged by the relegalization of liquor.

A Civil Works Administration provided many jobs through 1933 and 1934. None of the relief or recovery programs helped my folks or me. Yet we saw hope on more faces. My part-time employment was steady, though I moved around from part-time job to part-time job, from company to company.

In 1935 the Works Progress Administration became the Works Projects Administration and had the widest effect. Through it, I started my first full-time job, a career position as a secretary in a new Department of Works in Worcester.

Mama and Papa were ecstatic and gave praise and thanks to the Lord for answered prayer. God has an eternal perspective. His timing wasn't my timing. I was learning about patience. Long-time Worcester residents staffed the new works department.

A few men there knew my father. The other secretaries were young, new to their career, except Mrs. Maxwell, the head executive's secretary. She welcomed every newcomer, gave a tour of essential areas, and a pep talk about expectations in the work place. She enjoyed giving this talk. I could tell she was measuring the effect of her words and the listening skills of the new staff.

I was older than some and knew many techniques and tasks from my temporary jobs. I understood, coped, and organized anything quickly. I had a penchant for names and numbers that I had not used since high school. I surprised myself with what I remembered in an instant and impressed other people with my memory for details. Soon I was an assistant to Mrs. Maxwell and thus to the chief executive's office. I relaxed in the hope that my career dreams would come true.

Although I was happier and more secure, many people were still out of work. Families that had lived in Massachusetts for generations split as some left the state for work. Mama took food to many families and older people who lived alone. If people didn't have friends like my mother, I don't know how they survived the cold winters during those tough times.

Papa never worried about gas prices. We drove everywhere in our wagon, buggy, or cart. James drove dealership cars, and Ebba drove her own car. Hanne didn't have a car, but George taught her how to drive his. Even Axel knew how to drive, and he had a car! It amazed me to see that my little brother had a car.

Haime the-Jew had been at an auction where Axel wanted to buy an old Model-T that didn't run. Axel had only five dollars. Axel wanted its parts to fix Papa's tractor, a surprise for Papa. When the bidding went beyond his means, Axel left the auction.

The next morning, Haime towed the car into our yard behind his junk wagon. He had bought it for Axel. Haime said he did not know another young man so respectful of him or who would spend money to buy junk to help his father fix equipment. Haime was impressed with Axel's kindness and consideration.

I was not as mature as Axel. I was more selfish in handling money. I tolerated rules. How could I want so much? I lived with people who were content and thankful for what they had.

Axel wanted more, too. He talked about learning to fly an airplane. He said he'd own a car one day and buy me one, too. I reminded him that I couldn't work the foot pedals. He paused only a moment to frown, then assured me he could rig a car to work with hand controls. I never heard of a car equipped with hand controls, but I believed Axel could fix a car with equipment I could use. I could not even name all the equipment he had fixed or intriguing inventions he put together from junk.

I held on to a revived hope for many possibilities in my life. I would just continue to look for good opportunities and work hard. My doubts faded as my career blossomed. Compliments and trust came my way every day at the office, and they bolstered my hopes.

16

MOVING OUT, BECOMING PREY

"These birds[doves] are natural prey items in the wild and as a result have developed adaptations to reduce the chance of becoming the predator's next meal." **www.songbirdprotection.com**

In 1935 Axel graduated from high school as a top student. Instead of higher education, he chose to work at the Olson Company. Axel's excellent mechanical skills had been noticed by the various departments as they trained him. The managers watched in amazement at what he could do with equipment pieces. He was employed only a short time when he was called to repair complex equipment. If the managers saw Papa's tractor that Axel had fixed, they would have treasured and paid well to keep him as an employee.

My job responsibilities grew because Mrs. Maxwell liked me and groomed me to replace her. She would retire in 1940. Her confidence in me was tremendous. If I moved from home, I could focus more on my career. My parents

and Axel didn't understand that I wanted to live independently in Worcester, to go out with young people and not to
worry about transportation.

I wanted to make my own decisions, not be influenced by
my family. That was selfish, but I had faced that part of my
character long ago. As a responsible executive secretary, I
told myself that I should live independently.

For an easier transition, I looked for a room with a family
in Worcester, one attached with its own entrance. I told my
coworkers my desires. They each lived in different
Worcester areas, were my age, and got along well. They
helped me search.

After a couple months, one secretary strode to my desk
with a huge smile. "Annelise, I have the perfect place for you.
It's only a short distance from the Nazarene Chapel. It's an
apartment in the wing of a large, old house. Guess who now
lives there and will be your landlord?"

"Who?"

"The new pastor of the Nazarene Chapel!" "Are you
serious?"

"Yes. I looked at the apartment before I came to work. It
is wonderful. I'd live there if I hadn't already signed on as
Susan's roommate. It's one level, two rooms, and a bathroom.
A full bathroom with an indoor-plumbing toilet, sink, and a
low, new-style porcelain tub, not an old claw-foot
monstrosity."

"Oh, Patricia! That's wonderful! I'll go right after work."

"Here's the address."

Patricia left a slip of paper on my desk. Relief flooded me.
Mama and Papa would feel good about my renting a space
from a pastor and his family. The day seemed longer than
usual as I waited to go see the apartment.

We didn't have a full bathroom at home. Axel and Papa

talked about installing one. It would be a treat to live with indoor plumbing, but I didn't say that at home.

Like his father, Axel did piece work for other companies for extra money. He had hopes and goals he didn't share with us and often sketched ideas for inventions. Axel didn't gamble and always wanted to earn more money. His starting wage was thirty-five cents an hour in 1938. He worked ten-hour days, five hours on Saturday. He earned time-and-a-quarter after forty hours. I hoped Axel would one day earn what he was worth.

Finally, my work day finished. I took a cab to the minister's address. The pastor's wife greeted me and told me the apartment wasn't rented. She introduced herself as Beverly Cledwyn. Her husband was the Reverend Karl Cledwyn. She was a sweet-looking person, beautiful, big, blue eyes with thick lashes, no makeup, no fashion hairstyle. Her thick hair was honey color. Her skin looked bloated, but she was obviously pregnant.

I introduced myself as a church member and explained I had attended the Nazarene church soon after the church had started. We stood there in the front hall long enough for me to tell her what I did to earn a living and a little bit about my family in Holden.

Then she invited me into the main house, a typical, large, block house with four good-sized downstairs rooms, and an entry hall. Upstairs she told me there were four bedrooms. One for her and her husband, one for their two boys, one for their two youngest girls, and one for their teenage daughter. Beverly didn't look old enough have all those children. She looked tired. She was obviously pregnant again. I wondered about her life.

"Annelise. Did you say that was your name?" she asked as she took a key from the wall plaque filled with keys.

"Yes. A-n-n-e-l-i-s-e. Annelise Joren. J-o-r-e-n. It's a Danish name. Both my parents came to the United States from Denmark in the 1890s."

"Oh. My husband is Norwegian on his mother's side. His father was Welsh; that's why our last name is Cledwyn."

"And what about you?" I asked.

"I'm English. My family name was Bishop. I have a cousin who traced our family records back to the late 1600s in London."

"Do you have family in this country?"

"I have family here. Some are in the Bangor, Maine area. Others live in the South, in North Carolina. I rarely see them. We have lived in four different states since we married eighteen years ago. Maryland is where our eldest child, Katherine, was born. Our sons were born in Connecticut, and Rhode Island was the state where our youngest girls— the twins—were born. The twins are six and in school all day. I am beginning to feel like myself again. God is gracious since I'll have this new baby in a few months."

She led me into their house. "My husband, like most pastors, is busy with the needs of the flock, so I have to care for the children on my own. When he's new to a church, he has to make many calls to get acquainted, hospital calls, evangelism calls, and counseling calls. I know he feels torn between time given to the church and the time he would like to give to his family. He helps with discipline. Fathers are good with that."

"Hmmmm. I guess so. Do all ministers tend to move so often?"

I saw plain, well-worn furniture.

"In my experience, ministers' careers are either stay for twenty years or move every few years. My husband's a mover. I never know what sets him looking. I'm sure God guides him, and I follow. I'm good at packing up a household. I like this place, and Worcester seems like a great little city in many ways. I would like my children to go to school here. I hope we stay for a few years."

We went through the kitchen, out a mudroom like a small porch, and into the back yard. Hedges embraced the back yard for privacy. A variety of trees and flower beds landscaped the area.

"You must be a wonderful organizer to move a household with so many children, and to be settled in so quickly, Beverly. The last time we moved, I was about first-grade age. That was a lot of work, even with helpful neighbors."

"It is a lot of work, and I don't have the energy I used to. That's another reason I would want to stay for a longer while now. Come along this path. It goes through our garden, past this hedge . . . oh, I'm sorry! Is walking on the uneven turf difficult for you? You look so fashionable. I was impressed by your outfit and didn't notice until now that you have a limp."

"A limp?" I laughed. No one had ever described my lopsided walk as a limp. She was either extremely tactful or had bad vision.

"Beverly, I had polio when I was a toddler. I frequently sway like a ship hitting a dock, and that's not at all fashionable."

She laughed at my joke, then became serious "Oh, don't be hard on yourself, Annelise. You are lovely. Your dark hair and eyes, strong profile, high cheekbones, lovely natural pink lips, and perfect complexion . . . with those attributes, what person would notice a limp? I am surprised you are not married. Do you want to marry?"

"I think you've been generous in your review, Beverly. As for marriage, it might happen one day."

"I am the mother of a teenage girl who always questions

how attractive she is. I have learned to note and point out people's good features, to encourage them. I am usually too tired to worry about my looks. Perhaps when all my children are in school, I'll discover new energy."

"Being a good mother is a demanding job. I know. I have a great mother."

"You are smart, as well as attractive, Annelise."

"Thank you."

"You're welcome. Here we are. This door goes to the apartment's main room. It is . . . well, look yourself."

"Oh, it's big enough to be a kitchen and sitting room. I never expected so much space." I was flabbergasted with the apartment. It was far beyond my dreams of an apartment.

Beverly explained, "We were told the parents, who originally built this house, gave it to their son and his family. They added this on for their parents' living space. Look at the sink, counter, and cupboards. It's all newer than in the main house."

"It's wonderful!"

I stood inside the door. To my right was an attractive, almond brick wall with a fireplace. All the walls were painted a deeper almond. I would find decorating easy with a basic color. My mind already visualized enhancements for the apartment.

Directly across was a bay window with a wide window seat. To its left was the L of a kitchen area. Lots of cupboard space abounded. The oak cupboards were double-deckers, a row on the wall above the counter and a row beneath. The golden oak wood complemented the hardwood floor. The counter tops were a green-gray marble and easy to clean. A doorway stood to the left of the short part of the L. The wall to my left was plain with one sixteen-pane window.

Beverly stood in front of the sink and pointed to her

right. "The bedroom is through there, and the bathroom is beyond the bedroom. There's a walk-in closet so big it's like another room. The other door is at the end of the closet and goes onto a slate walk way to the street. An odd entrance, but it was an entry way for the older couple who lived here, not a closet. You'll probably use that the most. Of course, if you visited us, you would be welcome to go out our back door to this entrance."

I walked with a smile past her, hoping my desperation for this apartment didn't show. The bedroom had a sixteen-pane window on my left and my right. The wall directly across was plain. The bed head would go there. On the left was another door. I walked to it on the beautiful hardwood flooring.

The bathroom floor was made of sky-blue linoleum with flecks of white and dark blue. The walls were painted light blue. The toilet, pedestal sink, and low oval porcelain tub were white. A small window, high over the toilet, provided natural light.

I turned away from the bathroom and crossed the bedroom. The space was wide enough for a double bed, dresser, chair, and desk. Wonderful space, and well furnished, I walked into the large closet, almost a third the size of the bedroom. Two long dowel rods were on both sides of the walk-in closet. The couple had each claimed one side for their clothing and personal items.

The tiny alcove had enough space for a coat rack, an umbrella stand, and a small throw rug in front of the door. If someone came in with muddy feet, this little area would be easy to clean. I would place a thicker rug by the door so people could wipe mud or slush on it.

As soon as I opened the solid door to the outside, I saw the path of blue-gray slate that curved past low hedges and flower beds, then to the street. All the flower beds needed attention. I wondered if Beverly would let me plant flowers in those areas.

"Oh, Beverly, this has more space than any apartment I've seen. It's more than I dreamed I'd find."

She said nothing, just stood looking at me. I tried to sound calm when I added, "I would love to rent this from you if you would have me for a neighbor."

"Shut the door, neighbor," she said sweetly to me. "You're letting in the cold air. I think it might rain later. I want my renter to stay warm and healthy."

Beverly Cledwyn looked kind and welcoming. I treasured my good fortune. I would have hugged her if I had known her longer. That moment I was elated. Though I hadn't met her husband or children, I was sure I would get along with them.

The future looked brighter that afternoon. Mama and Papa would cope with my move better, knowing I rented from a minister and his family. This apartment had to be an answer to Mama's prayers for me. I had been praying with doubts. Mama prayed believing God would guide and provide.

I gave Beverly a deposit. She said it wasn't necessary, but I insisted. I felt more secure that the apartment was to be mine. As I splurged on a cab home, I felt lighter, even in my heart. I felt like I could skip, even fly with happiness.

If the future had been revealed to me at that moment, if I could have seen what was ahead for me in that house, would I have changed my mind? I think I would have run as fast as my gimpy leg let me, but I'll never know.

~

EBBA WAS the only one happy for me as I planned to move to the apartment. My parents were relieved it was in a pastor's home, but they wanted me to stay in their home. They would have been content for me live with them always. Axel was sad to see me leave because he would be the only child at home. He was a young man, thinking about his future and looking for a girl to marry.

Axel helped me move and brought in new purchased items, thus saving me delivery charges. I bought a carpet for my sitting room and a small, drop-leaf kitchen table of the same oak as the floor. Four chairs went with the table.

My most expensive purchased item was a double bed. I had never slept in a bed by myself until Ebba married. With the bed to myself, I decided if I lived on my own, I would buy a double bed. The headboard was cherry wood in a sleigh style, a style that looked modern, yet classic. My preferences for appearances usually combined those two characteristics, modern but classic.

The first evening I met Beverly's family after Axel and Papa had arranged my furniture and gone. I was in my work clothes, a costly outfit of a flattering, bright-colored jacket, white blouse, sleek dark mid-calf skirt, and patent shoes. Making a good first impression was important, and I walked slowly because that underplayed my crippled gait.

Beverly greeted and introduced me to her eldest daughter, Katherine, 15. She was a pretty girl with long honey-colored hair and her mother's blue eyes. The two boys were two years apart. Thomas, 12, had blond hair and brown eyes. Philip, 10, had brown hair and brown eyes. The fraternal twin girls, Abigail and Addie, were six with curly red-gold hair and big blue eyes. They all came forward to shake my hand.

Their father—the new pastor—entered the room.

Reverend Karl Cledwyn drew our attention. He wasn't a handsome man but had broad shoulders. He looked like the most masculine pastor I had ever seen. He stood over six feet with thinning dark brown hair and moved with casual assurance. Daunting in a dark blue suit, he looked over everyone in the room. Karl Cledwyn had gold flecks that sparkled in his dark brown eyes and a smile that fit a man who enjoyed life.

I felt a strange clutching around my insides. Nothing about his smile at me seemed pastoral. This was not the man of the house I had expected. A quiver trembled behind my breast bone. I thought it was heart palpitations of nervousness and hoped no one else could tell I was shaky.

Beverly, though obviously tired, beamed at Karl. She took his right hand. "Karl, this is Annelise, the charming young renter I told you about."

He smiled down at Beverly, and then he looked at me, directly at me, into my eyes. As I extended my right hand, he shook mine. None of them saw the instant electrical current between us. I felt so surprised, I might have gasped. I had never imagined a bolt of physical attraction like this would ever touch me, and certainly not from a pastor, a married man with a family. I *should* have pulled my hand out of his quickly and looked away from his face.

The children scattered to their seats around the table, except Katherine, who helped Beverly with the meal. Beverly and Katherine went back and forth from the stove to the table a few times. The younger children sat quietly, and Karl smiled in a way that reminded me of a lion, a kingly beast who could take whatever was in front of him.

I *should* have left that house that night. I *should* not have wondered what other feelings Karl Cledwyn could produce in me. I *should* have wanted to protect his wife and family. I *should not* have dismissed the physical and emotional charge that had run through me. I *should* have prayed to the Lord for forgiveness for lustful thoughts. I *should not* have told myself if I could control any passionate ideas or actions. I *should* have done these, but I didn't. I was hypnotized by a sudden glimpse of what I had longed for and never known.

The lustful appreciation and estimation in Karl's eyes petrified me. I would have stood like a statue except that Karl took my left hand with his right arm around my back and led me to my seat at the table. His arm around me exuded warmth wherever he touched me. Katherine held my chair for me. Beverly was already seated, tending to the little children, encouraging them to wait quietly for their father to sit down and say grace.

As I sat down, Karl squeezed my hand. My hand and heart throbbed while he moved to his place at the head of the table. There he smiled benignly on us all. I looked directly into his eyes. He returned my stare with his own look that was a challenge and a promise. Then he prayed, "Let us thank God for this wonderful meal, for the hands that prepared it, and for our sweet new friend and renter." Karl's voice was a melodious.

The whole family listened with eyes closed and head bowed, except for me. His voice was powerful even when he spoke softly. He had a hypnotic cadence that soothed. Surely, he would keep attention when speaking from a high pulpit in front of a congregation.

I tried to sort through my emotions, but my brain seemed frozen. What was it that hypnotized me? I never sat feeling helpless and confused with any other man. Why did this man make me feel weak, warm, and enticed to temptations I had not bothered to imagine ever before? Why does the prey stand motionless while the predator moves to pounce?

17

SENSITIVITY, ADDICTION,
EVASION

"Although considered a migratory bird, the mourning dove is actually a dimorphic species; one segment of the population migrates-and the other does not. Important factors need to be considered in order to understand the spectrum of why contradicting behaviors can dramatically vary within a species." **www.savethedoves.com**

I n 1940 after I had lived in my apartment over a year, Ebba said, "You're turning into a real livewire, Annelise."

Ebba's words were not a compliment. About once a week I had dinner with Ebba and James, or I just had dinner with Ebba if James worked late. Ebba was sweeter and more naïve than most women of thirty. She lived simply, but she wasn't simple.

Because of her own faith practices, prayer Bible reading, service to others, worship, Ebba was more sensitive to changes in me than Mama. Ebba had faced many more modern life situations. Mama was sensitive to people's needs, and continued over the years to help the poor and sick in her community, but Mama could be harshly stern with people who chose a life of sin. Mama could shut such people out, like the church groups that practiced shunning.

I had never seen that sternness in Ebba. I had seen resolve, perseverance, and love. Ebba might not have facts to support her intuitive knowledge, but she caught the right sense of any situation mighty quick.

Ebba and James had attended the First Baptist Church in Holden for the past year. Now Mama, Papa, Axel, Ebba, and James worshipped in Holden together. I knew the family felt pleased to have James and Ebba with them every Sunday.

When I asked Ebba why she returned to Holden, she said something prevented her spirit from worshipping with joy and openness at the Nazarene Chapel. She had discussed her feelings with James, and he followed her desires to leave the Nazarene Chapel. I wanted to ask her what made her uncomfortable where she had once felt spiritually refreshed. It was difficult, but I did ask.

"Annelise, I don't know. I sat for several Sundays wondering if I was getting ill or feeling too judgmental."

"You weren't ill."

"True, but I did feel judgmental. No matter how I tried to ignore it. Something about the new pastor, Karl Cledwyn seemed like the core of what bothered me. Once Pastor Cledwyn had preached for a few weeks, I just did not feel God's spirit in the sermons. Other people seemed happy, but I felt more miserable every Sunday even though you and James were there."

"Ebba, Pastor Cledwyn is a wonderful preacher. Everyone learns from him."

"He says good words. His speaking voice is strong, deep,

attractive. He knows the Bible, and his singing voice leads everyone wonderfully."

"But?"

"I can't be more specific Annelise. I just didn't *feel* right under the leadership of Karl Cledwyn." In spiritual matters Ebba had always followed the inclinations of her spirit because she believed it was the leading of God's Spirit.

Treading lightly, I inquired if her feelings had anything to do with my renting the apartment. She said no, but her mouth gathered like an old prune.

"Does my being so active in the chapel distract you?" I asked her. I played piano for hymn sings, played offertories, sang with the choir and solos. Ebba said no again, but her lips stayed tightly pursed. I stopped asking questions and tried to quell my guilt over my relationship with Karl, which had grown from the first day we had met.

No one, not even I, could count the times he had traveled the short distance through the privacy of the backyard to my apartment door. I never locked that door. It was wrong, but it happened. And it continued like an addiction.

I had met alcoholics. Addictions ruined lives, but addicted people continued to crave what was their downfall. I knew God existed and could free me from my addictions and sins, but I could not bring myself to lock the door even though I thought about it every day.

Someone at work once joked that if a person was not enjoying their sins, they were doing the wrong ones. I lived with misery and guilt in spite of my lively façade. I could not leave the Cledwyn home, though every day it crossed my mind that I should. If I was really an independent woman, how could I have let myself become addicted to a man who I should not ever see privately?

I didn't want my passionate relationship with Karl to

stop, even though I felt guilty after each stolen time. With a new baby boy, Beverly was oblivious to life outside her children. I was sure one of the children would notice that Karl and I seemed especially close as friends, but no one did.

Though I didn't want to be exposed for a fallen woman under the sway of an unscrupulous man, there were many times I wanted to stop the relationship. The weight of guilt oppressed me. I was perky and outgoing, but I was miserable inside. I knew I should not love another woman's husband, and I did not want to hurt Beverly. I thought I should despise Karl for taking advantage of my desires, but I was as guilty as he.

"Annelise, did you hear a thing I just said?" Ebba's voice held a rare sharpness.

"I'm sorry. I was distracted."

"Humph. You've been odd at listening since you moved from Bailey Road. Maybe all your late nights and parties with friends are catching up with you. How can you be active at church when you use all your spare evenings with friends? Mama and Papa told me they've wanted you to spend time with them, but you're always too busy. How many dinners have you have had with them in the past year? They miss you. Don't you know you're hurting their feelings? Don't you want time with Axel? That young man has done more for you over the years than any brother, older or younger could have done."

"Ebba, right now—"

"What? What good excuse can you give for ignoring your family? All you do is work, participate at church, practice for church, go out with friends, and stay at your apartment. They sound like good activities. Time with your family should be in there. Hanne and George spend more time with Mama and Papa than you do."

I knew my relationship with Karl was destroying my relationship with Ebba and with my family. I felt as though everything was closing in on me. I told myself that guilt would always be stronger when I spent time with anyone who could make me feel guilty. This whole conversation was the kind I had been dreading. I had to get out of Ebba's house and presence. I did not know when I would return.

I EVADED EBBA FOR A MONTH. Each time Karl and I were together, the passion was greater than before. What could come of our sinfulness? Why did his touch, smell, and feel overwhelm my thoughts and emotions? I had been raised to know and believe that nothing could be hidden from God. One's sins were bound to come out. I decided it would be best to live day to day, refusing to worry about the future. Avoiding home meant avoiding people who made me worry and feel guilty.

News of the family reached me through Ebba. Axel had a serious crush on a Miss Lise Thorsen. Ebba said she was a tiny beauty. She expected Axel would marry Lise. The family liked her very well. When this news didn't send me rushing to make plans to spend evenings with my family, Ebba grew more annoyed with my emotional distance.

I knew I was afraid they would sense my sin and force me to confess. What would they think of me? I didn't want them to know. I wanted my family to be proud of me.

How could I have allowed myself to have an illicit relationship with a married man, and that man a pastor? Was that many times worse than a regular affair? I didn't think God rated sin. God was concerned when people broke his commandments, but still loved them. People rated sins. I might as well sew a scarlet letter on every one of my outfits if people learned of our affair.

Now, in the spring 1940, I hadn't menstruated since December. I couldn't tell if I was pregnant. Some women were irregular for many reasons. I hadn't seen a doctor for anything over the years except my crippled leg and some bad colds.

What if I was pregnant? Would I tell everyone Karl Cledwyn was the father, or would I keep that to myself? I couldn't destroy Beverly and the family. I would have to keep the father a secret.

18

THE WAY OUT

"The **Mourning Doves** Coo may sound sad, but it can be a signal of the dove beginning its nesting habits of claiming territory, calling a mate, laying eggs, and raising young. The cooing sound is also where they get their name. Doves are a unique species when it comes to nesting." **Wild bird watching/Doves**

How would I feel about having a child? Some moments I wanted a child. I thought I'd like to be a mother who didn't have to consult the father or share the child's upraising. I had decided marriage was not something I craved. Women were supposed to marry, but I didn't want anyone having control or a say over my choices. Even my addiction to Karl had changed. After just a year and a half, our physical relationship seemed more routine than passionate.

Men did not fulfill women in most relationships I'd seen. Ebba wasn't in tune with James like Mama had been with Papa. Hanne was more distant from George. If I couldn't have what my parents had, I didn't want marriage. Even if I found a wonderful man, and if I tried to have a traditional marriage, a solid marriage like my parents, it would be a lie. Karl had ruined me. No relationship with a man would overcome memories of what I had experienced with choosing to sin with Karl. Even if God forgave me, and I had bee taught God would forgive if we asked, I could not erase the hours with Karl.

Mama had been a virgin, and I expect Papa had been, too. What decent man would want a cripple, who was not a virgin? I didn't look thirty-five, but I felt it. I had managed to remain slim, but if I was pregnant, that would change.

I went to Ebba's home. She was putting together a chicken pot pie. She offered me tea, and I sat at her kitchen table. I ran my hand over its surface. I remembered she had purchased it and much of her furniture with the remainder of the accident settlement. That seemed ages ago. Ebba made plans and stuck to them. She was deliberate, cautious, dependable, a treasure for James and anyone who knew her.

"It's good to see you., Annelise. You look a little tired but stylish, as usual. I like your hair up like that," Ebba told me as she finished the pie.

"You look good, too, even covered in flour to the elbows."

We laughed.

"I'll be done in a moment and sit with you."

I sipped my tea and watched her until she slid the pie in the oven and came to sit across from me. She had a mug of tea and put milk in it, English style.

"Is that something new? Putting milk in your tea?" I asked.

"I like it this way."

"Are Mama and Papa still just drinking Postum?" "Yes. I doubt they'll ever change."

"Ebba, I need to tell someone my secret, but it must remain secret, perhaps forever. I—I want to know if you still feel close to me, so close that I can tell you a worry on my heart. I know we haven't had many sisterly conversations in the past couple of years, close ones where we could say anything, but I could use someone to talk to like that now."

"Annelise, haven't I always kept your confidences? Haven't I always been a loyal and loving sister---except of course when I chose to elope. That was probably selfish, but I think I would do that again."

"Yes Ebba. Yes, you have been loyal and loving, and the elopement is something of the past that I don't think about now."

"Well then . . ."

I reached across the table with both hands and took hers.

I looked her right in the eyes. "Ebba, I might be pregnant."

Ebba didn't move. I doubt she immediately comprehended what I said. She stared as if her brain was having difficulty making sense of my words. Then a deep blush started on her neck and rose up the sides of her face. She understood and knew what I said and what that meant. She didn't know what to say.

"Ebba?"

"Annelise, . . . how . . . when . . . when will you know?" "I haven't menstruated in three months. I have been intimate with a man, but I don't feel like I am very different. How does a woman really know she's pregnant?"

"Annelise, who? Who is the man, the father?"

"I don't want to say."

"How can you drop this on me and not tell me the father?"

"If I am not pregnant, then everything will be fine.

Honestly, I have thought I would like to have a child. I earn enough that I could hire child care and . . ."

"And nothing! Annelise, what is wrong with you? Are you demented? I can't believe you would choose to raise a child alone! How can you choose to be a parent on your own? Is that fair to the child? You sound so selfish? Are you sincere or is it just because you think you are pregnant? I don't think parenting alone is what God intended."

I straightened up and said, "Lots of things in life are not what God intended, Ebba. You know that. Can you forgive me?"

Ebba pulled her hands from mine. She reached one shaky hand out to pick up her mug of tea. She lifted the mug to her lips and sipped slowly while staring at me. I saw tears in her eyes when she spoke to me.

"I would forgive you, Annelise. Of course, I would forgive you for making a mistake. We have had discussions about the mistakes, the poor choices people make. We are not above making those choices. We all sin. Having a child will be difficult for you, but you have overcome so much. I am sad that you might have to face the situation of being an unmarried mother!"

She watched me and tears filled her eyes. Then she reached one hand to cover my hands. "I understand you are a passionate person. Everyone wants to be loved. I wish you could have the relationship God intended for intimacy. Oh, Annelise, if you are pregnant . . . is there any chance he would marry you?"

"No."

"Positively?"

"Positively."

"Why? Do you still see him? Are you still intimate with him?"

"Yes."

"Then there's a chance he might marry you. He must care about you."

"He will not marry me if he cares about me."

"But how can you be . . . Oh, dear Lord . . . he's already married?"

"Yes."

"Annelise!"

Ebba let go her mug of tea, put both her arms on the table and rested her head on them. I couldn't tell what she was doing. She made no sound. When she lifted her face, she was pale and looked like she might faint.

"Ebba, drink some tea. Is there sugar in it?"

She shook her head from side to side. Ebba stared at me with a sadness that caused her blue eyes to become so full of tears they spilled over her face.

"Ebba, I never imagined that I would have a relationship with a married man, but. . ."

"Never mind what you imagined. Never mind what you have done. You must end it now. End the affair today. It's fornication and adultery. It's awful, just awful. Think of his poor wife."

"But Ebba . . ."

"How can you even begin to argue with me, Annelise?" She wiped at her tears.

"Because I can't imagine cutting myself off from him. I don't know how. Sometimes I want to, but then he will do or say something so it seems he needs me."

Ebba sipped her tea and then put her hands in her lap. "Is it your boss, Annelise? Tell me that, please. Is it your boss or some other man with power at your office?"

"No."

"Good. You can end it then and keep your job. You have

such a good job, so much hope for the future and career. Don't throw it away on some adulterous man."

"I haven't thrown anything away."

"You have thrown your moral values away. When you did, you threw away pieces of yourself. Annelise, think of what Jesus said to the woman caught in adultery. 'Go and sin no more.' You can be forgiven. Just end it."

"It's not like that. If you knew . . ."

"Nothing would change my opinion. It isn't good for your soul. You have to stop. You can stop. You are strong-willed. You could stop right now. How long has it been going on?"

"Over a year."

"Oh, my!" Her eyes overflowed with more tears. Ebba grabbed the mug. Then she sat, holding it like a life support, staring at me and crying.

"Ebba, I am sorry I upset you. I shouldn't have said anything. I should have waited until I knew for sure about the pregnancy."

"I . . . I am just dumbfounded . . . just dumbfounded."

"Forget I told you," I threw that thought at her and started to rise.

"Ridiculous. Sit down." She motioned with her hand. "What a statement to make: to forget it. To my dying day, I won't forget this conversation."

I went around to her and kissed her forehead. Then I gathered my purse and jacket. "We won't talk about this now, Ebba. I love you, and I appreciate what you are feeling, but I can't talk about this anymore. I am just so tired. I cannot argue more. I can't end it."

"Annelise."

"I'm not staying. Please don't say anything to anyone else, not to James, not to anyone. I don't know why I told you. I should have waited until I knew for sure about being pregnant."

She followed me to the door. "I know why you told me. You feel guilty. You want it to end, and you need help. You know what you have to do. I will do anything to help you. Can't you please tell me who it is so I can help you end this affair? You will be miserable—body and soul—until you do end it. I am sure you know that."

"Maybe you're right, Ebba, but I don't want to talk any more now. I shouldn't have burdened you. It is my problem. You're a wonderful sister even if I'm not."

I left her little house quickly. She was right. I was tormented with fear and guilt. Yet I wanted to return to my apartment. What would I do or say when I saw Karl? I couldn't imagine telling him we would never be intimate again.

TWO DAYS later Ebba sat in my kitchen when I arrived from work. She stood at once. She held a fierce expression on her face. I felt like I was looking at a wrathful angel. Her eyes blazed electric blue and did not waver or blink as she stared at me.

"Ebba! What a surprise! How long have you been here?"

"I arrived a few minutes ago."

"Did Beverly let you in?"

"She escorted me through their kitchen, out their back door, and in your door. She said with the backyard so private, neither of you locked the back doors."

Ebba kept staring at me while she explained this. Why was she upset that we left our back doors unlocked? Few people in decent neighborhoods locked their doors.

"Annelise, I will help you pack. You can go home to Bailey Road, come to stay with James and me, or stay with one of your friends, but I am not leaving here, not today, without you. *You are leaving here immediately.*"

"What is wrong with you? Ebba, how can you tell me I must leave my apartment? If you're worried about what I told you, forget it. I'll be fine."

There was no evidence yet that I would be fine. I dropped my purse on the table and limped to put the kettle on the stove. A cup of tea always made me more energetic. My period hadn't come yet, but I felt no unusual internal changes. It had to be stress, not pregnancy.

"I am not blabbering to hear myself talk, Annelise. *I know.*"

Her words were clear but I went to the stove to start a kettle of water boiling. She came to the stove, turned the burner off, and said with a intense whisper, "I know who the father is."

"What?" Her tone registered. I looked at her and realized it was true. She knew who I was having an affair with. I didn't know how she had found out. Yet the answer was simple, so innocently discovered, and so like Ebba

"I was worried about you. I went to see *your* pastor at his office. The secretary wasn't in, and the office door was open, so I knocked on it. He said, 'Come in,' and I did."

I leaned against the counter for support. I felt faint with horror and shame. Ebba had gone to Karl. She had heard directly from him.

"The truth shines out from your pallor," she told me. "If I hadn't known for sure, If I had not been able to believe it, I would now. This is awful. I read Elmer Gantry the same summer you did Annelise. Never, never would I have dreamed I'd encounter such a supposed man of God. God help him. And God forgive me for hoping Pastor Karl Cledwyn has some punishment for taking advantage of you."

I felt paralyzed. Elmer Gantry, Ebba compared Karl to Elmer Gantry. Elmer Gantry was the shocking opportunist whom people believed was a man of God. Sinclair Lewis had written the Elmer Gantry story about a religious charlatan and manipulator. Readers were shocked and entertained. We read the book and hoped our parents didn't know. Now, my sister wasn't entertained by fiction, just shocked by the reality of me and Karl.

Ebba wrapped her arms around me and held me while she told me the rest.

"I marched right into his office. I had no idea, Annelise, no idea. I went to him because pastors are people we can trust. My intention was to get immediate help for you. I said, 'Hello, Pastor Cledwyn. I am Annelise Joren's sister. I can't believe what I have to say to you.'

"I paused then because I couldn't imagine how to tell him. He stood up. He lost all color in his face. I hardly noticed that. Nothing would stop me from trying to get help for you.

"I blurted out, 'My sister told me . . .' and then I stopped. I couldn't speak. It seemed impossible to tell your pastor and ask for his help. I thought about how I should word it. I could only stand there staring at him with the pain I felt for you and tears in my e yes.

"I thought I would have to reveal your terrible secret to him. Pastors hear such things in confidence, so I didn't consider it as breaking your confidence. I was frozen, paralyzed by not knowing what to do, and yet I wanted help for you."

Ebba took a slow deep breath. "But before I said anything else, he spoke. He spoke quietly and seriously. He thought I knew, and I did not even guess until he looked right at me and said, 'Don't judge Annelise too harshly. I'm twelve years older and have a family, and I couldn't stop the attraction between us.'

"I nearly died, Annelise. My heart thumped so hard I thought it would come out of my chest, but in the next instant, I felt my heart had turned to iron. My lungs stopped. I don't know if any blood pulsed through my body. I gasped. My face must have said it all because suddenly he realized I hadn't said *what* I wanted to talk about. His guilt and God made him speak, made him tell me.

"I understood. His words, his voice, his face. How could he? I am amazed God doesn't strike him dead in the pulpit. How can he take advantage of you and dare get into the pulpit? How could he have let this happen? How can God let that man keep preaching?"

Ebba was right. In his guilt Karl had assumed too much when Ebba blurted out, my sister told me. He felt guilt too and assumed she had come to confront him. Ebba could fill in the blanks. She still had come to my apartment now determined to rescue me.

I hugged her. "Maybe no one ever made him memorize Numbers 32:23 at the early age Papa made us memorize it. *Be sure your sins will find you out,*" I muttered the words.

Ebba looked clean and smelled new, fresh, like when she was a baby. She might be married, but she was an innocent. I loved her so much! Why had I chosen to give in to Karl's advances? Why had I continued?

Be sure your sins will find you out. When I acknowledged those words of scripture, they calmed her. God knew everything. In one way or another, our sins come out in knowledge, consequences, or health.

Ebba said a faint, "Yes." She held me at arms-length. "You are leaving this place today. By God's grace, I pray you are not pregnant. I pray you can separate from this awful man who took advantage of a romantic lonely young woman under his roof, abused a sweet woman, his own dear wife, his children by not loving their mother faithfully, and betrayed his congregation who trusted him.

"Say you will come with me now Annelise. Promise me that you will not return. You can do it. I'll help you. You can make the right choice."

I didn't move or say anything. Inside I trembled; outwardly I wilted.

"Please, Annelise. I beg your sensible, strong-willed self to remove yourself from this house." Ebba looked into my face. She burst into tears and great gulping sobs.

I hugged her. She seemed more shattered than I. It was time to act right. I left after packing two cases of clothes while Ebba collected toiletries and small personal items.

We went to Ebba's house because I didn't want Mama or Papa to know. James knew only that I was upset over a broken romance and needed to stay with a close family member for a while. James was kind to me, but I wondered how he would act toward me if he knew about my affair with Karl. Would Ebba ever tell him? Could I ask her to always keep it a secret even from her husband?

I stayed a month with Ebba and James. Ebba drove me to work but would not drive me to the Chapel. I still attended and played the piano at the Nazarene Chapel. I didn't know what Karl was going to do or say. If I changed my entire routine, people would notice my absence and ask questions. I also wanted to hear what Karl said on any of the Sundays after I disappeared from his house and home life. Beverly and their children were not in the next Sunday morning worship service. My heart clutched with pain at what Beverly lived with in her deceptive husband.

The Reverend Karl Cledwyn, the next Sunday, announced his resignation. I sat cold as an icehouse. He looked calm and normal as he told the congregation he felt led of the Lord to move. He said he and his family would leave in a few weeks, that he was sorry his time with the chapel had been so short, but that God's time was frequently on a different schedule from human time.

Shivers rushed through me at the announcement. I forced myself to look at him like the rest of the congregation was looking at him. Karl didn't look at me. If we were in the same area, his eyes slid by me. He never spoke with me again. Perhaps Ebba's prayers created a shield around me so I wouldn't. Sometimes I wanted to force him to speak to me about the affair, but other times I was thankful not to talk with him.

I only talked with Beverly as I packed my remaining things. Axel and Papa brought our big wagon to pick up my furniture. I prayed they would never discover the truth.

Beverly was kind to me. Talking to her was difficult. Guilt clawed at me all the time we talked. I prayed Beverly's heart would withstand it if she discovered her husband's infidelities. I prayed their family life would survive. I prayed the children would listen to what their father preached rather than to follow him in breaking God's commandments. I could not bring myself to tell Beverly about my affair with her husband.

Beverly had tears in her eyes as she told Ebba and me about the new move. I was polite with no extra conversation. Guilt overwhelmed me in her presence. If she didn't know about her husband's unfaithfulness, I would not tell her. If she knew and could not face it or confront him, I would not make her feel more guilty for tolerating his adulteries.

My pain also involved my loss of independence. A piece

of my life was forever marred. Something wonderful had been spoiled. I reaped the consequences. God had heard my words of repentance and forgiven me, but the inner scars lingered with memories I could not erase. What I had done might fade through time, but the imprint of my sin would always be in my mind.

By the end of the month Karl and his family moved. He didn't have another church, but someone said he and his family went to stay with Beverly's parents until he could find his next pastorate. I wondered how many virgins Karl had overwhelmed with his attention. I doubted I was the first. He was far too authoritative and confident in his approach and words. I felt foolish, demoralized, and empty. My menstrual cycle started. Not once, ever again, did I experience an irregular period until I hit the change of life.

19

PENANCE, GENERATIONS, AND LOSS

And Jesus said to his followers, 'Behold I send you out as sheep in the midst of wolves; so be wise as serpents and innocent as doves.' **Matthew 10:16**

I n the spring and summer of 1941, Holden had many special events for its Bicentennial. World War II was fought on another continent. In our little place, people lived in peace and safety and were glad to celebrate their town's 200thbirthday.

The main celebration was held in May. Ebba sang with the combined church choirs, over one hundred voices. Since I was one of the charter members of the Nazarene Chapel in Worcester, I anticipated attending the Chapel into my old age, until I could no longer manage to go. However, memories led me to not sing in such a joyful public time as the combined choirs at the bicentennial celebration.

Each service was a penance for me and a lancing of a spiritual boil. It was painful, unpleasant, and necessary. One day I hoped the poison effect on my soul would be gone. I listened differently and looked into faces carefully. I wanted to know people in more than surface relationships, but disappointment in myself led me to spend free time alone. I wondered how many people struggled with hidden sins and lived in pain.

My piano playing added to the Chapel services. People commented with those very words many times. Every Sunday, someone thanked me for playing. Now I used my musical abilities to return to people I felt I had robbed because of my actions with Karl Cledwyn.

Ebba and I never talked about the affair. Sometimes with her arm around me or her visit to my new apartment, she was just what I needed. God gave me Ebba as a gift. She had strength in her petite frame, in her love, and in her soul. No other person—even my parents—gave me the peace Ebba did. Waves of shame swept over me at the thought of my sin exposed to any of my family other than Ebba.

Hanne and I were friendly but not close. I knew I was jealous sometimes of her. She was fully a part of the family. Her nursing career thrived. George was financially well off, and life was good for Hanne and George.

We noticed the men in our lives more after December 7, 1941. No one dreamed of an event like Pearl Harbor. By spring, most people knew we had a family member who would enter the war. I worried about Axel and the young married men with no children.

Young men disappeared from every community. Surprisingly, Axel did not have to go to war. His skills were essential to the war effort, so he was told to keep working on the machines and parts. He wished he could fight the enemy, but our family and friends wanted him home. He put in extra hours making the twenty-millimeter shells. Often his brain was in high gear inventing changes and improvements for equipment, processes, and fuses.

Every able person enlisted to help the war effort in some way. When Mrs. Maxwell retired, I was promoted and given more responsibilities. I focused on work plans in those crucial war years. No standing around and chatting in the offices. People felt compelled to work hard, even to look for additional work they could do to help employers and the country.

Every business functioned differently in wartime. Everyone realized doing their job and living conservatively were critical to the war effort. We learned about the armed services, war industries, registration sessions, civilian defense programs, air raid observations posts, emergency squads, volunteers for the fire departments, economic restraints, and rationing for such items as sugar and gasoline.

With the Depression over, Worcester and Holden had blossomed into growing communities. Many groups at our church worked on projects for the servicemen. Voluntary saving defense funds were collected. Books were sent to the Armed Forces. Women's church societies knit blankets, socks, and sweaters for the servicemen. Food was shipped to Britain and Holland.

A spirit of camaraderie and service to a great cause grew. When we heard service men and women were wounded and killed, sadness touched us all. We grieved even with strangers. When good things happened, everyone celebrated in moments of joy.

Ebba didn't call me a live wire any longer. I stayed a social creature, but never again had an illicit relationship. I loved to flirt and was not offended when men flirted bac It was a friendly game, nothing serious, a distraction to bad news we all feared. I wanted nothing beyond that from any man. The men I met recognized that I was not looking for romance.

Although I loved to socialize, at work each promotion moved me to become more business-like. I could be curt, authoritative, and remote. I used that executive secretary demeanor as a wall against the few men who did make advances beyond mild flirtations.

I didn't consider marriage or engage in conversations about my ideal husband with unmarried women. I wanted to be admired, but not accountable to any man. I sometimes still longed for my own child and I thought about adoption, but I wasn't ready to be a parent.

Ebba and James adopted a five-year-old girl in 1944. Her mother had a rough life often living by desperate measures, but they told no one except me. They had wanted children. Year after year Ebba had been disappointed when she did not become pregnant. She had a couple of early miscarriages, but she was not bitter. I didn't know how James felt because I did not talk with him and I never asked Ebba about James. Anything I learned would come from what she chose to share with me.

Hanne and George had a child. They seemed to be a happy little family whether at planned family times or whether we had a spontaneous visit. I did feel happy for them.

Axel married his heart's love, Lise Thorsen, a soft looking but strong girl from a good Danish and Christian family. Lise had the skills Mama had as a homemaker, from making curtains to jams. Lise even played the piano and her parents would give Axel and Lise a piano for their home. Our parents were happy as their children moved forward, but especially joyful to them was that Axel and Lise would live nearby on Bailey Road. They were a devoted hardworking young couple, as so many were through the war time.

The war ended with V-J Day, September 2, 1945. What relief we felt! Towns and cities held welcome home ceremonies and memorial services. Service clubs were formed, new housing developed, populations doubled, and new areas developed as couples built homes outside the cities.

Holden's population increased at a faster rate than neighboring Jefferson. The town of Holden changed with the constant multiplication of businesses along Main Street, but it was still a small town compared to Worcester. Any day I journeyed to our farm, I felt like a time traveler, stepping back in time. Memories stretched along the road.

At work my responsibilities grew, but I kept up. I also established a lively pace and jovial patter in the office.

My boss told me, "I don't know how I managed without you, Annelise."

Other people from coworkers to clients were also complimentary of my efforts. For some of the tense demanding years we started early or stayed late. Commuting was difficult for me and no car service was available for employee transportation.

Our company only used a car to pick up packages. My boss was a creative problem solver. He trusted me with paperwork and laborious complicated forms, and he wanted a way to guarantee I could arrive at work when the office opened and stay as late as necessary. He arranged my transportation via the company car by listing me as a package to be picked up or delivered. The surprise I felt at my package identity made me laugh.

Through the late 40s and early 50s, my boss and company took good care of me. They were especially careful during winter ice and snow. My heart and soul were soothed to be so appreciated.

The company Ebba worked for closed due to mismanagement, but she quickly found new employment in Worcester. Her adopted daughter had behavior problems from tantrums as a child to staying out overnight without telling Ebba or James. As usual, Ebba was hopeful her daughter would develop and make better choices. We all prayed for that every day.

Our family gathered regularly on Bailey Road. Mama and Papa loved having us there. Mama had slowed down. We pitched in, glad that running water and indoor plumbing were now in the house. Papa still had no desire to own a car.

At one July fourth gathering, Axel gave me a stunning gift, his spare time project: a car equipped with hand controls. I had confessed to Axel driving was a desire of my heart, and it felt good to say the words out loud, even if an impossibility. Axel hadn't laughed at me.

He told me he wanted to attempt to make such a car. I said I'd pay the cost for materials. Axel had stored parts and worked on it in one of Papa's sheds, telling only Mama and Papa about the project. Now I was dumbfounded. Axel had created a car equipped with hand controls.

Everyone agreed he had outdone any previous mechanical designs with the hand-control car. Hanne doubted I could manage driving even with hand controls, but Ebba and James encouraged me.

I had my first lesson that afternoon. What a feeling of freedom that car renewed in me! I was almost 45 and just learning to drive a car, but I felt young.

Axel was a good instructor. He gave clear directions, was patient, and had a quick sense of humor about my mistakes while encouraging me. He knew I was overcome at the magnitude of his gift. I cried tears of joy and thankfulness during our driving lessons.

I said through tears, "You are a super brother and must be the greatest husband and father. Axel, you have blessed all our lives many times over. Thank you!"

In a short time, I was parking *my* car at the curb outside my Pleasant Street apartment building. I no longer was a special package for pick-up and delivery, except in the worst weather. I could now offer others lifts when I went to supper with friends. I could take day trips with friends and sometimes when she could get away for a day, with Ebba. The next half dozen years were some of my best at work, with friends, and with my family.

Sometimes my driving speed bothered Ebba. Usually she'd say something like, "Oh, Annelise, I think you whizzed right by the road you wanted!"

I was amazed I could zoom along and frighten my otherwise imperturbable younger sister. My fears had decreased except for fear that remained after a tornado invaded our area.

In 1953, June—a tornado—came with horrifying power and speed. I had never heard of a tornado in our area. It swept through our region on a Sunday afternoon. The reservoirs fed the tornado with moisture.

We heard later it had first hit in Petersham then sped on to tear up parts of Rutland, Holden, Worcester, Shrewsbury, Westboro, and Southboro. Assumption College in Worcester lost its main building. The damage was assessed at millions of dollars. The 90-minute twister killed almost 100 people and over a thousand people had serious injuries. Investigations showed that more than 9,000 people were homeless.

F-4 Tornado hit Worcester County, June 9, 1953.

My apartment, street, neighborhood, and office building were not touched, but whole Holden neighborhoods were demolished. Communities throughout the state aided our county. Three major roads were blocked by debris: Main Street, Holden Street, and Brattle Street. I trembled and was literally sick with worry until I heard Bailey Road had been spared, and my family was safe.

Crews worked round-the-clock to clear debris and fix power and electricity. People without homes found friends and relatives to shelter them. The Red Cross and churches provided meals, clothing, and aid. National guardsmen protected areas from looters. A curfew went into effect.

The following year we suffered two more rare disasters. Hurricanes hit our area. Hurricane Carol arrived in August, and hurricane Edna swept through on September 11, 1954. Edna seemed worse, perhaps because we hadn't recovered from Carol. Religious folks talked about end-time signs. Carol dumped six inches of rain on central Massachusetts. Edna added six more.

Lyon Street, Worcester, after Hurricane Edna, September 1954

I had coffee with Ebba one evening when we heard more active hurricanes would hit our area. Less than a year after Carol and Edna, we suffered a deluge from both hurricanes Connie and Diane. I hugged Ebba tightly before I left. Too many days I took Ebba, my family, and friends for granted.

Forty percent of downtown Worcester was flooded in the battering storms of 1955. I was thankful to live on a high, dry street. I never had to pass through the flooded areas to work. My whole family was spared damages. A mixture of relief and guilt motivated us to help families for months after the storms.

Storms do not just come through weather. A variety of storms had hit our family's spirits too. The loss of Ingelise shocked our family. Her letters had come more frequently and were warmer over the years, but she had never come home to know her brother. Now she was gone from this world.

Then another shocked and crushed our souls. Mama died. She hadn't been sick and never complained. We didn't run to doctors. The only times we needed them were during my illness as a baby and Ebba's accident with the furniture truck.

Suddenly Mama was not with us. We couldn't absorb it. Everything at the farm said she was there. The funeral and burial in Holden took place. Papa assured us he was fine on his own. None of us believed that. I shivered thinking of him alone in the house.

He and Mama had been close in heart and mind for over sixty years. How does someone live alone in a house after sixty years with a loved one? How does someone crawl into a bed that sags in the middle because of hugging a loved one there every night for decades? How does one carry out daily routines without feeling an overwhelming loss of a life partner?

AXEL'S CHOICES, PAPA'S DEATH

"Life Span of a mourning dove show that free-living doves
live between 7 and 11 years of age. However, banding
research confirms a longevity of much longer than that.
The mourning dove is actually one of the 10 longest lived
free-living species holding a record of 31 years 4 months."
Songbird Protection Coalition

The children and grandchildren were attentive to
Papa. Finally, Axel and Lise and their children
decided to live with Papa on Bailey Road. I blessed
them for that. I would have been horrified to move back to
Bailey Road. My worst fears of my youth would have overwhelmed my heart living out the prescribed life for a cripple.
That's what people expected I would do.

Axel soon built a new spacious ranch house a stone's
throw from the old farm house. He and Lise and their children had their own space and modern conveniences while
keeping Papa company each day. Axel's innovations and

creative ideas made the new house snug and welcoming, spacious, and charming.

He worked in hours to help Papa renew the fruit trees and bushes. The peaches, raspberries, apples, blackberries, blueberries, and pears flourished with Axel's care more than they had with Papa's. The property increased in value through the years and through the high-quality fruit the farm produced.

One evening I stood by the apple trees overlooking the yard and fields that had been so deep with snow that only our neighbor, with a huge Belgian work horse, could drag a V-shaped wooden plow to clear a path. I wondered about the choices I made when I was young. Now, I was content with my career and friendships, but what had I given to my family?

I looked at the house to see Axel's youngsters playing in the backyard. They laughed and hollered without inhibition. I resolved to live more thankfully and to visit Papa at least once a week. That could improve my relationships with Axel's family too. Stopping my jealous and negative thinking seemed necessary. I must move away from the oppression of meanspirited thinking. I longed to focus on what was good, like Axel did.

One time I confessed to Ebba that I was jealous of her easy relationship to Axel's family. His children seemed casual and affectionate with Ebba. She moved with ease and tenderness even though her own child had given her frequent heart breaks. I clomped into their living room, spoke firmly, moved with some difficulty, and didn't have much patience with children. In retrospect I knew it was good that I had not chosen to be a single parent.

Ebba gently told me that Axel's girls didn't understand Aunt Annelise. They knew their father and mother loved me dearly, but I was critical. I tried to think of ways I had been critical, words I had spoken harshly and hastily.

That had been my problem since I had taken a leadership role in my company. I did not suffer foolishness and quickly to point out something that could be improved. Perhaps my quick judgments about people, politics, decorations, houses, or even their parents had been made in the presence of Axel's children.

They had visited my apartment and with delight lowered and raised my Murphy bed. They were surprised to shouting out loud and laughing when I first pulled it out of the wall. They seemed at ease. The oldest told me I was pretty. I remember these compliments because children are most honest people. The younger girl told me my eyes twinkled.

The asked if they could try on some of my clothes. It was as much entertainment for me as it was for them to see them put on a fashion show in my regalia. Without Mama to sew for me, so skillfully imitating the latest fashions, I tended to buy the most stylish items I could afford in hats, jackets, dresses, cloaks. Only my shoes didn't fit their play as I had special adapted shoes for my different size feet.

Had I been negative when Axel's girls had come to my house? Sometimes when I was negative, I was joking. Sometimes I was just in a bad mood, but how would children know the difference? They took words literally.

Axel's children loved their aunts and spent more time with Hanne and Ebba. It was foolish to be jealous of their attachments. If they did not know me as well as Hanne and Ebba, that was my fault.

When I had free time, I went on trips alone or with friends. I felt some guilt at choosing travel over time with family, but. I couldn't imagine relinquishing trips until I was old, poor, or feeble.

Standing before the Statue of Liberty was one of my travel highlights. I remembered my childhood fascination with Emma Lazarus, memorizing her poem for the statue and our country. I realized too late that I could have offered to take nieces with me on my travels. I could have taken trips and still made sure to spend more time with my nieces and nephews, and over the years with grand-nieces and grand-nephews.

In the late sixties James died of a heart attack. We supported Ebba in finances and visits. James did not have any life insurance and spent liberally on cars and clothing.

Papa's words comforted Ebba. He reminded her that in the thirty-one years she had with James, she had been loved. James's family loved Ebba. She told me though she didn't spend much time with them, they made her feel important in their home. His mother said James had found a treasure in Ebba.

Proverbs 31 described the ideal woman. I thought Ebba had most of the qualities of the treasured woman, and thought I might have a few. "A good wife who can find? She is far more precious than jewels....Her lamp does not go out at night. She puts her hands to the distaff, and her hands hold the spindle. She opens her hand to the poor, and reaches out her hands to the needy. She is not afraid of snow for her household, for all her household are clothed in scarlet. She makes herself coverings; her clothing is fine linen and purple. Her husband is known in the gates, when he sits among the elders of the land. She makes linen garments and sells them; she delivers girdles to the merchant.

Strength and dignity are her clothing, and she laughs at the time to come. She opens her mouth with wisdom, and the teaching of kindness is on her tongue. She looks well to the ways of her household, and does not eat the bread of idleness. Her children rise up and call her blessed; her husband also, and he praises her: "Many women have done excellently, but you surpass them all. Charm is deceitful, and beauty is vain, but a woman who fears the LORD is to be praised. Give her of the fruit of her hands, and let her works praise her in the gates."

We learned during the repast after the funeral for James that Papa had required Axel to memorize Proverbs chapter 31. Papa wanted Axel to know what to look for in a wife. Poor Axel had to memorize lots more from Proverbs that we girls never had to learn. Proverbs is filled with warnings to young men about thoughts, actions, and the lure of loose women.

Axel memorized texts quickly. He had found in Lise a Proverbs woman. Not Ingelise, Hanne, or I could come close to being the ideal woman of Proverbs, but I knew my mother, Ebba, and Lise suited all the best attributes described in Proverbs.

At the start of the 1970s, Papa left us. His death came suddenly but quietly while he sat in his favorite chair. His Bible was on his lap when Axel found him. Papa had seemed in good health all the time. His looks had changed, but his spirit was youthful. Hanne, Ebba, and I were shocked and could not think of what to do without his quiet guidance. Even when we disagreed with him, we knew he had a sure foundation for all his beliefs and opinions.

Grief overwhelmed us. Axel and Lise ended up handling everything. Axel's reserves of strength surprised me. Lise was gracious to help us through our grief.

Once again, I found myself not just grieving over a person but over the passing of a way of life. The immigrants had formed America's cities, railroads, industries in ways early colonists never attempted. They appreciated America's opportunities. What would happen to America when the entire first-generation immigrants had passed? Papa and Mama symbolized the best of immigrant hopes, goals, and efforts to me. Papa made me comfortable with calling God, *Father.*

Axel asked if anyone wanted to move into the old homestead. When none of us wanted to, he said he would sell it and divvy up the proceeds. That sounded fine to me, but not if the buyers would tear it down. Axel assured us he would find people who would value a historic home. He would retain all property except the yard to the farm house. Papa had left the property to Axel in a will. We girls knew Papa trusted Axel to care for us and since he was the youngest of us, Papa expected Axel would outlive his elder sisters.

Retirement years neared for me. A nest egg from the proceeds of the farmhouse sale would have been helpful. Unfortunately, I had not saved a large amount from my share of the sale of the homestead. I had not spent cautiously. I had nothing on credit, but I had saved only a little. My trips were indulgent in hotels, restaurants, and activities. Clothes and hair salons also took money from each pay check. Axel advised me about investments, but I did not learn to value his investment advice until many more years passed.

Hanne, Ebba, Axel, and I accepted being orphans. We were thankful we had each other. We gathered regularly on holidays. We dropped in for casual visits, too.

Frequently when her only child had left the home, and not on good terms, but after arguments and heartaches, Ebba would stop by to visit me. One day she dropped by while I was dressing to go out with friends.

"Ebba, will you bring me my red wool jacket from the closet?"

She left to fetch it and called from the bedroom, "Which one?"

"What do you mean, which one?" I called back angrily surprised by such a foolish question. I gave a more specific description. "The red wool jacket with the black velvet collar and covered buttons."

I bought several new outfits every season. Ebba returned to my living room laughing, then frowning, and holding two identical jackets. She shook her head.

"Whatever will I do with you, Annelise? You probably should catalog your clothes. You didn't even know you had two jackets the same."

I was annoyed that my mistake amused her. It had never been comfortable when my younger sister sounded more mature than me.

"Annelise, Axel's girls asked me if I had seen your rainbow of sweaters. I told them you loved color and style. But two jackets alike. . . you need to purchase clothes more carefully. You leave me dizzy with your impetuous decisions."

I looked at Ebba and wished I had her sense and sweetness, but I didn't. Probably I never would, and she loved me anyway. She loved me in spite of all my bad decisions. I took the jacket from her, and we hugged.

"I love you, Ebba. You are the best sister. Sweet as a songbird and wise as a fox."

"Indeed? Well, I like that combination." She laughed again and helped me by holding one of the red jackets so that I could slide my arms into it. "And what are you, dear older sister? Would you describe yourself as bird or beast?"

"I'm late. I'll leave it to you to figure that out Ebba."

CHARACTER, JEALOUSY, RETIREMENT, SECOND MARRIAGE

"Give ear to my prayer, O God; and hide not thyself from my supplication. Attend unto me, and hear me: I mourn in my complaint, and make a noise. . . My heart is sore pained within me: and the terrors of death are fallen upon me. Fearfulness and trembling are come upon me, and horror hath overwhelmed me. And I said, 'Oh that I had wings like a dove! for then would I fly away, and be at rest.'" **Psalm 55:1-6 (KJV)**

"I never thought I'd reach old age," I told Ebba in the middle of playing one of our weekly scrabble tournaments. She laughed. Scrabble was a popular game in our family.

"Annelise, how could anyone imagine living into old age when they have lived through a crippling disease, a society that made no allowances to help handicapped people for far too long a time, a depression, a wrong romance, wars, rationing, tornados, hurricanes, blizzards, the 60s, gas embargos, the 80s celebrating greed, and now wars and rumors of more wars? You have lived through so much, dear sister. You should *expect* to live to 100."

"I didn't, and I don't. Ebba, I want to have a serious talk with you."

"Remember the day I came to play Scrabble, and you were in pain from that fall when you slipped on the patch of ice?"

"Oh, don't bring that up again."

"Why not? It shows your self-judgment is impaired. You were so good in business. So many heart-broken people sincerely missed you when you retired! They thought the place would collapse into confusion."

"That was a backhanded compliment. If I did a good job training my replacements, they should have known I would be leaving them with people competent to keep everything running smoothly."

"Do you hear what you just said, Annelise? You said *replacements*. They had to hire *three* people to do what you had done with apparent ease all by yourself. You had to write a manual and to train your replacements in the details for three areas.

"It just baffles me. How can you be capable in one arena and incapable of taking care of yourself? I found you limping from a fall on the ice, and then you talked me into playing Scrabble! Then, after beating me, you realized you were in terrific pain, and at the hospital, they discovered you'd broken your leg."

"It was a hairline fracture."

"You'd broken your leg, your good leg, and you wanted to just ignore the pain and to play Scrabble," Ebba emphasized.

"Winning always made me feel better."

"And it still does. You should be happy now. There is no

way I will win this Scrabble tournament. It's late, Annelise. I should go. There's a biting chill in tonight's air."

"Ebba, do you know what I'd like for a nice home-made snack before you go?"

"Snacks? Annelise, you should not eat at this time of night. That is why you put on weight."

"You didn't let me tell you."

"Tell me." Ebba picked up the Scrabble pieces.

"I'd like Mama's homemade donuts."

Ebba looked as though I'd asked for strychnine. She put the game on the shelf and picked up her jacket.

"Annelise, those donuts tasted delicious. But they were fried in a bucket of fat."

"Weren't we healthy back then eating all the baked and fried goods Mama made?"

"Oh, you're hopeless." She gave me a kiss. "Good night, sister dear." Ebba went to the door and in a minute more she would be gone. I needed to ask her a question that was always in my thoughts when she came to mind.

"Ebba, can anyone help you with Rene?"

Rene was Ebba's grown daughter, and she was a mess. Ebba had been with me for hours this day and other days in the week, and I had been too timid to bring up any areas of pain. I had not brought up the subject though it had been on my mind constantly.

Ebba had always wanted children. Before she married James, she used to tell me how she wanted at least four, probably six children. She wanted a family like Mama and Papa had.

How did Ebba stand the disappointment? She had invested years in loving her child, providing for Rene at sacrificial cost, and nothing had helped Rene stay on the straight and narrow. Many parents faced the same situation.

I listened when people talked about the heartbreak that came from the bad choices their children made. Hearing such grim stories helped me feel more at peace as a childless woman.

"Annelise, several people and agencies have tried to help me with Rene, but no one can help her right now. She has to want to turn her life around. I have turned her over to the Lord. It will take a miracle for her to repent and change the direction of her life. I'm glad James didn't live to see her like she is now."

"I admire you, Ebba. You have always been able to forgive and love people even when they make awful and foolish choices."

"We can have a mutual admiration society, Annelise. Now look, before I go, I want to encourage you to think about Axel's suggestion. You shouldn't live on your own through another rugged winter. We are concerned about you. There are lots of assisted-living choices in Worcester now. We, Axel and I together or separately, we'll take you to visit each place so you can decide."

"I'm only five years older than you, Ebba."

"Annelise, there's as big a difference in a person over 90 and one five years younger. Look how much children change between birth and two, between two and five. You're 93. I'm a spring chicken—not quite 88—compared to you."

"Okay, spring chicken. I'll think about it," I said that so she wouldn't worry. I'd been in and out of hospitals several times in the last few years. Ebba had worried or phoned or come by each day for more than a decade.

I was fine at first after I retired in the mid-70s. Forty-four years given to the Massachusetts Department of Public Works as an executive secretary after I passed those starting years of trial and error, interviews, and layoffs. I had a good retirement fund but I wasn't thriving financially like Axel.

My! That man could invent, invest, and see amazing growth with sales of his inventions and his careful study of the stock market.

After Ebba left, I thought about the joy travel had given me, but should I have sought marriage? Did I miss not being married and not having children? Sometimes I did. I wondered how many years I had left. My health had been like a roller coaster once I hit ninety. Ebba was right about certain ages being a turning point.

In my 90s I had reverted to the pudginess of childhood. I had put on weight. That wasn't healthy for one who gimped around. Since I left my eighties, I'd enjoyed eating more than I enjoyed new clothes. Little held me back from food indulgences. My looks were not a concern. The years of wearing sophisticated suits and perfectly matched sweater-skirt outfits had passed.

I didn't take trips or attend plays and events with friends as I used to because many of my friends were in worse health than mine or dead. My only outside responsibilities were playing as the substitute pianist at the chapel I still attended occasionally. Ebba rarely visited the chapel with me. She preferred attending worship services in Holden with Axel and his family.

Pudge, the name made me smile now. Once I had hated it. I was pudgy and why should that bother a ninety-three-year-old woman? Certainly, arriving sane and healthy to one's nineties was an accomplishment. Sometimes I tried to diet, but it didn't work for long. Nothing matched what Mama had baked but I did enjoy treats.

Ebba on the other hand was as trim as the spring chicken she claimed to be. She moved lightly, and her figure was almost youthful. Her smile was youthful, and her spirit in spite of everything she'd been through, was young.

Ebba had a second offer of marriage. In 1982 she married Jared Branch, a widower from church. My! He had pursued her. He knew she was great wife material. Ebba never held out against a determined person. Not a shred of romantic love ran between them, but they enjoyed each other's company. They respected one another. She would have loved more years with Jared Branch, but a heart attack robbed her of another husband when they still were in their newlywed year.

And how long had Hanne been gone? A heart attack had taken her too. Must be a dozen years. As Hanne and I aged, we were at ease with one another. Heart attacks. They ran in our family. Would that be my fate? It was late and cold. Time to turn up the thermostat if I stayed up to watch television. I didn't feel like reading.

What should I do? Assisted living? There was a lovely apartment complex not far from my Pleasant Street apartment. Axel had taken me to see it and explained I'd be fine financially. If I chose assisted living, Axel would move my things. He'd arrange everything.

He'd also offered for me to live with Lise and him. Their children were grown and living spread out from Maine to Georgia. I knew that as long as I could cope financially, I wanted to live independently.

Ebba and Axel appreciated antiques. Axel had a number of the larger furniture pieces from Mama and Papa while Ebba had the cane-bottom chairs and the wind-up wedding clock from Denmark. The family history lived with them every day of their life, but I had Mama's piano. At family gatherings, Axel and Lise's grandchildren asked us older adults questions; I felt like they saw us as talking antiques. I didn't enjoy being an historical object.

James and Ebba's adopted daughter had troubles all her

life. They had tried to help her and always forgiven her and taken her in when she came to them for help. I saw God in the way Ebba coped with her unbalanced daughter. From God's perspective, I must be a lot like Rene. He loved me and waited for me to realize I needed Him.

I did feel tired. Perhaps I would go to bed. In the morning I planned to tell Axel I'd move into assisted living. That's what I thought before a stroke in the night robbed me of choices. A series of mini strokes kept me under the care and decision-making power of others. I knew I had to get stronger or others would choose where I ended my days!

22

BEYOND THIS WORLD

The dove often a symbol of innocence prompted Christ to advise his disciples to be aware of the evils of the world. When sending them out, he warned them: "See, I am sending you out like sheep into the midst of wolves; so be wise as serpents and innocent as doves." **Matthew 10:16**

"Ebba, assisted living was heaven compared to this place! I want out of here. I want to go back to an apartment of my own," I told her as adamantly as I could.

My sister looked pained as she did whenever she had to argue with anyone. I saw her find determination. "Annelise, you have to stay in this rehabilitation home until you . . ."

"It's a nursing home. Call it what you want; it's a nursing home. Look out the windows. What do you see? A boring parking lot. No one feeds my mind or soul. Half the people are senile, and that includes staff! I want to leave."

"Physically you need more help than we can give you

Annelise. You need the help of the professional staff here a while longer."

Ebba looked toward the door and then smiled. "Here comes Axel. He can explain it to you." She looked relieved at his presence.

I turned and looked directly at Axel's steely eyes. There were times when Papa peeked out of Axel's eyes. He was prepared to stand against my pleas. He did not like it when I caused Ebba any stress because she had always tried to make life easier and better for me. Little did he know the secrets of my life that Ebba had shared with no one.

"Axel, I want to leave here. This is the third time in a year I've come here. I want to go to an assisted-living apartment."

"This place is better than you make it out to be Annelise. We found the best place for you. You knew that when you came here. Your health needs are very complicated. We worry about you. You need day-to-day help. Even together, Ebba, Lise, and I can't take care of all the things you need. You have that help here, and they are good people. I checked this establishment out carefully before we registered you here." His face remained resolute.

"Axel, do you remember when you were sent to the cellar for punishment to think over what you had done?" I asked him.

"Yes, but what has that got to do with this?" Axel never wanted to stray from the subject. He often reminded me of a terrier.

"While you were down in the cellar, for a time of repentant, thoughtful punishment, you ate the peaches stored there."

"Sometimes Annelise you make the strangest leaps . . ."

"This place has nothing like peaches. Axel, if I am to be

punished by being in a nursing home, I want some treats, not this place."

"Be reasonable, Annelise. I'll bring you peaches, even chocolates. This place is warmer and brighter than the cellar where I had to think over what I had done. It had a dirt floor and huge spiders hiding in the crevices of those old stone walls."

His description was correct. Our old field stone cellar with the dirt floor had many spiders in the crevices between the stones. We laughed, and I felt better, for a little while.

AFTER TWO MONTHS in the nursing home, some of my strength returned. Axel and Ebba came to visit as regularly as the little figures who came out on some clocks to strike the time. They were delighted that I felt better. They never made me feel like a burden. I sat in bed and made normal conversation.

Then came a day when Axel had permission to take me out for a day trip. He, Lise, Ebba, and I took a fun full day tour down memory lanes. We visited all the places our family had lived since I had been born. What a day!

We drove through the southern part of Worcester County and imagined Papa covering those miles on a horse. We looked around Grafton where I had contracted polio. In Worcester we saw three-story family dwellings filled with children in the yards and old people on the porches. Listening to the children, we could tell the huge old houses were still filled by immigrant families, just from different parts of the world then when we had lived in this neighborhood.

Axel took us to lunch in a new Worcester restaurant near

the State Mutual Building. I had eaten at little luncheonettes as a Fairchild student. This restaurant had the environment my English friends would call posh. The ramp for handicap had the disguise of a red-carpet entrance giving gentle access. The host greeted us as though we were special guests.

In more wandering through Worcester, Axel took me past former places where I had employment. I saw no dress shops from my shopping spree days, but we did drive past the Nazarene Chapel. Axel asked if I wanted to stop there, but I said no. The day had been so good I wanted no return to regrets.

I did realize we hadn't visited the house where I had lived with the Cledwyn family. There was no way to know if this was an oversight or part of the day's plan. Could Ebba have told Axel about my greatest transgressions? I wouldn't ask either Ebba or Axel.

In the afternoon we wandered around Holden, past the Gale building where I'd worked so hard to become Valedictorian, past the Baptist Church Mama and Papa had enjoyed so much and that Axel, Lise, and Ebba enjoyed with the church family there now. We passed new stores and buildings that had changed owners and purposes. The old post office was now a barbershop. We saw a new grand and large Dawson School, wandered in a great loop up and down Reservoir Road, and drove into old and new neighborhoods from Holden to Jefferson to Rutland.

Memories overwhelmed me with images and emotions creating a churning blend of confused memories within me. Finally, I felt myself relax when we arrived at Axel and Lise's house. We rested there and ate supper. Lise had cooked a roast on a low temperature all day. She had home-baked bread like Mama's. The day and food brought tears to my eyes. We had our meal in a sun room Axel and Lise had added to their house.

After the meal, we looked down the hill past berry patches and fruit groves toward the old farmhouse. Axel pushed my wheelchair out into the pastel and golden evening. We watched the sunset over the Holden hills. When it was dark, we went back inside we looked at photographs of their children and grandchildren.

Axel and Ebba drove me back to the nursing home and escorted me to my room. I hugged them and gave them each a kiss. We were not a kissy-touchy family, but it had been such a special day! Their love had surrounded and strengthened me.

I said thank you, but that could not begin to tell them what the day had meant to me. That evening, Sophia, a kind aide, helped me into bed. She had emigrated from Ghana. I told her about my family as she helped me prepare for bed. She listened and agreed I was fortunate to have a caring brother and sister. She missed her parents, brothers, and sisters in Ghana. She missed the warm, sunny weather, the foods, and the language.

I asked what had brought Sophia to this country. With her family so far away and much warmer weather, why would she settle here in Worcester? Her husband, that's what she told me. She had come with her husband when he wanted to leave Ghana for America. I smiled, thinking again that I had made the right decision in choosing to remain single.

THE EUPHORIA from the trip kept me strong for almost two weeks. Then as quickly as I had improved, I weakened. Some days it felt difficult to lift my head. Ebba tried to explain the doctor's test results. I had multiple problems, affecting many organs. I wasn't even strong enough to hum favorite songs. But I did not feel alone.

The Lord and I had become closer since I lost my independence. Sometimes when I thought and prayed, I moved to new levels of remorse for my mistakes. Then I remembered I had confessed my sins, and God had forgiven me. I knew in my head I had been forgiven, but sometimes I didn't feel I had forgiven myself. So many of my choices had been selfish.

I thought of Proverbs 28:13, "He who conceals his transgressions will not prosper, but he who confesses and forsakes them will obtain mercy," or of First John 1:9, "If we confess our sins, he is faithful and just, and will forgive our sins and cleanse us from all unrighteousness."

I knew I had been promised forgiveness. I claimed that forgiveness. Christ had taken my sins on Himself on the cross so I could be free of them. How thankful I was to have been raised by parents who loved God and modeled His love for me. How thankful I was for the hope of eternal life. I would see my family who had gone ahead of me to heaven. I would see them all again, healthy, and rejoicing.

In my weak moments and dislike for living alone, I felt aggravated, then fearful, then bitter, then resigned, and finally impatient with the weakness that overwhelmed me. Everything was an effort. I wavered in and out of consciousness.

Since I'd been in the nursing home, I'd lost weight. The enforced diet had lessened the stress of weight, and I felt sapped of energy too. I had no strength for moving. I realized I would never leave the nursing home until I went to my home in heaven.

Facing that fact gave me pride in my ability to be realistic, yet at other times I became lost in memories, almost as if I was present in the past moments that came vividly into my mind. Sometimes I thought I sang hymns. But I didn't still have a voice did I? I remembered solos I'd sung in worship services and singing with the choir. I sang childhood songs. The songs filled my head and heart even if no one heard me.

I felt myself sinking in health and still was thankful for God's love. Would peace still fill my mind and soul when the Angel of Death came for me. I thought that angel could appear at any moment. Mama had told me once that even at the time of death, God showed His love for us by sending an angel to escort us home. I thought of the Angel of Death as a strong guardian escort, not a fearful creature.

It Is Well with My Soul, had impressed me when Mama first sang it. Mama told us the story behind the song. The writer of the words was a man who had suffered severe business losses in the Chicago fire. While settling his business affairs, he had sent his wife and daughters to England to visit family. On the journey to England, the boat sank. The man's daughters drowned. Only his wife survived. She sent him the awful news.

He traveled on the next boat to England. The captain told him when they reached the approximate place where the daughters drowned. There, the hymn's words came to him.

> When peace, like a river, attendeth my way,
> When sorrows like sea billows roll
> Whatever my lot, Thou has taught me to say,
> It is well, it is well, with my soul.
> It is well, with my soul, It is well, with my soul.

Though Satan should buffet, though trials should come,

Let this blest assurance control,
That Christ has regarded my helpless estate,
And hath shed His own blood for my soul.

My sin, oh, the bliss of this glorious thought
My sin, not in part but the whole,
Is nailed to the cross, and I bear it no more,
Praise the Lord, Praise the Lord, O my soul!

And Lord, haste the day when my faith shall be sight,
The clouds be rolled back as a scroll;
The trump shall resound, and the Lord shall descend,
Even so, it is well with my soul.
It is well, with my soul.
It is well, it is well, with my soul.

I felt Mama and Papa nearby. I knew when Axel and Ebba sat beside me, but I could not concentrate to have a conversation with them. I felt safe and loved knowing they were near me.

I drifted away from them. I looked toward other family members and friends I could see. At first, they seemed at a great distance from me. Then they became more visible. We would be together soon. I knew it.

I would hug Mama and Papa again, and I would be able to run to them! We would be together rejoicing with the Lord. I could feel a healing beginning, a tingling surge of energy removing all my illnesses, pains, old age, crippled leg, and twisted, shrunken foot.

Soon I would be free of painful memories. My voice would let me sing praises. My body would be whole as God meant it to be when I was born. I would have the motion and the wholeness I had longed for all my earthly life. I would know what it meant to be physically free. I would stand, walk, skip, run, and leap joyfully in an eternity of love.

AFTERWORD

Annelise's funeral service took place ninety-four years after she entered the world. The cover of the service booklet showed Psalm 139: 9–10: "If I rise on the wings of the dawn, if I settle on the far side of the sea, even there your hand will guide me, your right hand will hold me fast."

The text for her service was from II Timothy 4:6–7: "The time has come for my departure. I have fought the good fight. I have finished the race, and I have kept the faith. Now there is in store for me the Crown of righteousness, which the Lord, the righteous Judge, will award to me on that day— and not only to me, but also to all who have longed for his appearing."

Songs in her funeral service were "He Giveth More Grace," "Jesus Is Always There," "Faith Leads to Victory," and "It Is Well with My Soul."

Annelise's (Anna Nielsen) grave is in Holden's Grove Cemetery.

Ebba (Esther) and Axel (Anker), who spent hours talking with me about their family, hoped readers would see in

Annelise a wounded dove, a courageous character, the potential of all individuals, the ways people should empower those with disabilities, the forgiveness everyone needs, and the love of God through our lifetimes into eternity. Annelise faced struggles and disappointments but ultimately lived in the hope and promise of eternal life with wholeness, forgiveness, and love through Jesus Christ, the Lord.

If you enjoyed *Wounded Dove*, please tell others what you appreciated in a review on Amazon which automatically posts to Goodreads. Here's how you can do it:

1. Go to the product detail page or your order page for the item. Scroll down until you see the place (on left) for reviews.

2. Select **Write a product review** in the **Customer Reviews** section.

3. Select a star rating.

A green check mark indicates successfully submitted ratings.

4. Optionally, add text, photos, or videos and select **Submit**.

Thanks so much!

ACKNOWLEDGMENTS

This book would not have been possible without the information, journals, and conversations with Ebba (Esther) and Axel (Anker) Nielsen. Thank you to Pam Nielsen for your gracious encouragement with this revised second edition. The archives of the American Antiquarian Society and the Worcester Historical Museum provided details that enriched and affirmed Annelise's life experiences.

Ongoing thanks to my husband, Jerry, whose love and support makes my daily writing efforts possible. Thank you to my beta readers: Dr. Barbara Driscoll de Alvarado, Sloan Perron, Rev. Dr. J. D. Heslinga, Caryl Saunders, Lucinda Bradley, Sparkie Ciriacy, Elaine Mallory, and Lieutenant Fred Lussier, Massachusetts State Police (ret.). Thank you to Jim and Flo Munro and Sandy Kurtz for writing prods. Thank you to family and friends who have encouraged my efforts, the supportive community of Anna Maria College, writing groups like the national Flourish Writing Community, Must Love Words of Ashland, the Ashland Public Library, and my long-term writing friends in Advancing Writing Endeavors (AWE). Hearty thanks to the First Baptist Church of Holden, Massachusetts, and Holden's Gale Free Library for generously sharing their historical documents. Special thanks Carolyn Allard for editing. Broadest thanks to Rev. Dr. Gordon Saunders for cover and content design and mentoring me through revising and publication.

ABOUT THE AUTHOR

 Virginia Heslinga, Ed.D., is Associate Professor of Humanities at Anna Maria College in Paxton, MA. She received the Living the Mission Award, which is presented to a member of the faculty who understands and appreciates the great importance of educating the whole student and seizes every opportunity to do so.

Over 48 years, Virginia has taught in a variety of schools, public, private, alternative, homeschools, religious and online. She has worked in this country and in others with every age group. She has articles published in education journals, writes curriculum, and has a memoir, *Grace Interlaced*, about a fire that devastated her family and changed her life. Virginia is a child of God, a wife, mother, grandmother, educator, author, and traveler.

Virginia Heslinga